HOW THE MIND WORKS

CHRISTIAN D. LARSON

HAWK PRESS

Published by

Hawk Press

4836/24, Ansari Road, Daryaganj
New Delhi – 110 002
Phones : 9643330713, 91-11-23278618, 91-11-35676207
E-mail: thehawkpress@gmail.com
www.thehawkpress.com

ISBN: 978-93-88318-97-6

FOREWORD

Everything that is in action must necessarily work through definite laws. And as the mind is in constant action, alternating its actions at almost every turn of thought or feeling, it is evident that a vast number of laws are employed by the mental process. To know how the mind works, therefore, we must know something about these laws.

In the following pages the most important of the mental and metaphysical laws known to date are considered from every possible viewpoint, the principal object being to ascertain their real nature as well as their power and use. In addition, a number of psychological ideas are presented that will throw light both on the inner and the outer workings of the mind.

No effort, however, has been made to delve into the mysteries of the mind; this will be done in another work, the object here being to present the practical side of mental action, and present it in such a way that anyone may learn to use the powers of the mind properly. And at the present stage of psychological study, this is the most important. We want to know how the mind does work so that we may, in all mental work, use the mind in the best, the fullest and the most effective manner.

The fact that we have, in the past, known practically nothing about the real workings of the mind, and also that there are only a few minds, even in the present, that have gained the power to direct and control mental action according to system, design and law, should make the study of this book both interesting and profitable. In fact, we are convinced that all who understand the purpose and the message of this book will become highly enthused over its practical value; and will accordingly gain more from its perusal than tongue can ever tell.

That this number may be very large in the present, and constantly become larger in the future, is our dearest wish in this connection; for when you know that a certain thing is so very true and so very important, you want everybody else, if possible, to gain all that you have gained from the understanding and use of that particular thing.

And this is natural; we all want to share the truth with others; we all want everybody to gain that power through which the richest and the best that life has in store may be realized ; and this fact proves that there is far more of the noble in human nature than we have previously believed. However, it is only as we learn to use the mind in harmony with the natural and orderly workings of mental law, that everything that is noble in human nature will find expression.

CONTENTS

CHAPTER I.

THE GREATEST POWER IN MAN.

It is now a demonstrated fact that the powers and the possibilities that are inherent in the mind of man are practically unbounded. And this conclusion is based upon the discovery that no limit can be found to anything in human nature, and that everything in human nature contains a latent capacity for perpetual development. This discovery, and no discovery of greater importance has appeared in any age, gives man a new conception of himself, a conception which when applied will necessarily revolutionize the entire sphere of human thought and action.

To be able to discern the real significance of this new conception will naturally constitute the greatest power in man, and should therefore be given the first thought in all efforts that have advancement, attainment or achievement in view. The purpose of each individual should be not simply to cultivate and apply those possibilities that are now in evidence, but also to develop power to discern and fathom what really exists within him. This power is the greatest power because it prepares the way for the attainment and expression of all other powers. It is the power that unlocks the door to everything that is great and wonderful in man, and must therefore be understood and applied before anything of real value can be accomplished through human thought or action.

The principal reason why the average person remains weak and incompetent is found in the fact that he makes no effort to fathom and understand the depths of his real being. He tries to use what is in action on the surface, but is unconscious of the fact that enormous powers are in existence in the greater depth of his life. These powers are dormant simply because they have not been called into action, and they will continue to lie dormant until man develops his greatest power; that is, the power to discern what really exists within him.

The fundamental cause of failure is found in the belief that what exists on the surface is all there is of man. And the reason why greatness is the rare exception instead of the universal rule can be traced to the same cause. When the mind discovers that its powers are inexhaustible and that its faculties and talents can be developed to the very highest degree imaginable, and to any degree beyond that, the fear of failure will entirely disappear. In its stead will come the conviction that man may attain anything or achieve anything, provided, of course, he works within the natural sphere of universal law. Whatever circumstances may be today such a mind will know that all can be changed; that this condition can be made to pass away, and that the vacancy may be filled with the heart's most cherished desire.

That mind that can discern what exists in the depths of the real life of man does not simply change its views as to what man may attain or achieve, but actually begins to draw upon the inexhaustible power within, and begins at once to develop and apply the greater possibilities that this deeper discernment has revealed. When man can see, feel and understand what exists beneath the surface of his life, the expression of this deeper life begins, because whatever we become conscious of that we invariably bring forth into tangible expression. And since the deeper life contains innumerable possibilities as well as unbounded power, it is evident that when the deeper life is clearly discerned, anything within the human sphere may be attained or achieved.

The idea that there is more and more of man than what appears on the surface should be so constantly and so deeply impressed upon the mind that it becomes a positive conviction, and no thought should be placed in action unless it is based upon this conviction. To live, think and act in the realization of the fact that there is "more of me" should be the constant purpose of every individual. When this is done the more will constantly develop, coming forth in greater and greater measure, giving added power, capacity and life to everything that is in action in the human system.

When the average person fails he either blames circumstances or comes to the conclusion that he was not equal to the occasion. He is therefore tempted to give up, and tries to be content with the lesser. But if he knew that there was more in him than what he had applied in this undertaking he would not give up. He would know that by developing this "more" he positively would succeed where he had previously failed. It is therefore evident that when man gives attention to his greatest power, that is, the power to discern the more that is in him, he will never give up until he does succeed ; and in consequence he invariably will succeed.

That individual who knows his power does not judge according to appearances. He never permits himself to believe that this or that cannot be done. He knows that those things can be done because he has discovered the more which really exists within him. He works in the conviction that he must and will succeed because he has the power. And this is the truth. He does have the power. We all have the power.

To live, think and work in the attitude that there is more of you within the great depths of your being, and to know that there is more of you within the great depths of your being, and to know that this "more" is so immense that no limit to its power can be found, will cause the mind to come in closer and closer touch with this greater power. And you will in consequence gain more and more of this power. The mind that lives in this attitude opens the door of consciousness, so to speak, to everything in human life that has real quality and worth. It places itself in that position where it can respond to the best that exists within itself. And modern psychology has discovered that this "best" is extraordinary in quality, limitless in power, and contains possibilities that cannot be numbered.

It is the truth that man is a marvelous being, and the greatest power in man is the power to discern this marvelousness that really does exist within him. It is the law that we steadily develop and bring forth whatever we think of the most. We shall therefore find it highly profitable to think constantly of our deeper nature and to try in every manner and form imaginable to fathom the limitlessness and the inexhaustibleness of these great and marvelous depths.

In practical life this mode of thinking will have the same effect upon the personal mind as that which is secured when placing an ordinary wire in contact with a wire that is charged. The great within is a live wire. When the mind touches the great within it becomes charged with the same immense power. And the mind is more or less in touch with the great within when it lives, thinks, and works in the firm conviction that there is "more of me," so much more that it cannot be measured.

We can receive from the deeper life only that which we recognize, because consciousness is the power between the outer life and the great within; and we open the door only to those things of which we become conscious. The principal reason, therefore, why the average person does not possess greater powers and talents is because he is not conscious of more. And he is not conscious of more because he has not recognized the depths of his real life, and has not tried to fathom the possibilities that are latent within him.

The average person lives on the surface. He thinks that the surface is all there is of him, and therefore does not place himself in touch with the live wire of his great and inexhaustible nature within. He does not exercise his greatest power the power to discern what his whole nature may contain, and therefore does not unlock the door to any of his other powers. This being true, we can readily understand why mortals are weak. They are weak simply because they have chosen weakness. But when they choose power and greatness they shall positively become what they have chosen to become. And we all can choose power and greatness, because it is in us.

We all admit that there is more in man than what is expressed in the average person. We may differ as to how much more, but the more should be developed, expressed and applied. It is unjust both to the individual and to the race to remain in the lesser when it is possible to attain the higher, the richer and the greater. It is right that we all should ascend to the higher and the greater now. And the greatest power in man reveals the fact that we all can.

CHAPTER II.

THE BEST USE OF THE MIND.

We have at the present time a number of metaphysical systems, and though they differ considerably in many respects they all produce practically the same results. We find that no one system is more successful than the others, and yet they are all so remarkably successful that modern metaphysics is rapidly becoming one of the most popular studies of today. The real secret of all these systems is found in their power to draw consciousness more deeply into the realization of the absolute.

The absolute is unconditioned ; therefore the more deeply consciousness enters the absolute the less conscious will the mind become of conditions. That is, the mind will be emancipated more and more from conditions as it grows into the realization of that which is unconditioned, or rather above conditions.

Any method that will tend to develop in the mind the consciousness of the absolute will produce emancipation from physical or mental ills, the reason being that there are no ills in the absolute, and it is not possible for the mind to be conscious of ills when it is in the consciousness of that which is absolutely free from ills. In other words, the mind cannot be in darkness, weakness or disease when it is in light, power and health.

Although it is not exact science to state that all is mind, because it can easily be proven that all is not mind; nevertheless, the statement that all is mind has a tendency to resolve consciousness into the allness of infinite mind, that is, the mind of the absolute. This will eliminate from the personal mind the consciousness of personal limitations and thus produce the realization of the absolute, that state of being that is free from conditions. It will also cause the personal mind to function in the consciousness of its unity with the impersonal mind which again is the infinite mind.

In like manner it is not scientific to deny the existence of matter, because matter does exist. Nevertheless the persistent denial of the existence of matter has a tendency to eliminate from mind the consciousness of shape and form, also the limitations and the conditions of shape and form. The result will be a certain degree of emancipation from conditions, and accordingly the ills that may have existed in those conditions will disappear.

The purpose of metaphysical methods is to prevent superficial mental action by deepening thought into the understanding of real action; that is, to prevent bondage to the limitations of form by awakening the consciousness of that limitless Hfe that animates all form, and also to prevent the creation of imperfect conditions by producing in the mind the realization of absolutely perfect states. Any method that will tend to promote these objects in view will prove healthful to a degree in producing personal emancipation from sickness, adversity or want; but if the method is not strictly scientific its value will be very limited, and will prove to be nothing more than a temporary aid in the lesser aspects of life.

In this connection we must remember that no metaphysical method can fully promote the purpose in view unless it recognizes the reality of the whole universe and aims to produce advancement in every individual expression of universal life. However, every method is at first incomplete, therefore not strictly scientific. But to be scientific we must give everything due credit for what it is doing, no matter how limited it may be in its personal power.

To awaken the consciousness of the real, the unconditioned and the absolute, it is not necessary to declare that all is mind, nor is it necessary to deny the existence of matter. On the contrary, such methods should be avoided, because they will prove detrimental to the highest development of the individual if employed for any length of time. And we realize that our purpose is not simply to emancipate man from the ordinary ills of personal life, but also to develop man to the very highest heights of real greatness.

There is a world of absolute reality that exists within and about all things. It permeates all things and surrounds all things. It is an infinite sea in which all things live and move and have their being. It is the source of everything, and being limitless can give limitless life and power to anything. All science recognizes this world of absolute reality, and it is the purpose of metaphysics, that is, the best use of the mind, to gain that understanding that will enable any individual to place himself in perfect conscious touch with that world. This absolute reality is the perfect state of being upon which all individual being is based. Therefore the more perfectly conscious the individual becomes of the absolute, the less imperfection there will be in the life of the individual. And when individual consciousness is completely resolved in absolute consciousness, the cosmic state is realized a state with such marvelous beauty and such indescribable joy that it is worth a thousand ages of pain to come within its gates for just one single moment.

To develop the consciousness of the absolute and to grow steadily into the realization of the reality of perfect being the fundamental essential is to live habitually in the metaphysical attitude. This is a distinct attitude, by far the most desirable attitude of the mind, and comes as a natural result of the mind's discernment of the existence, the reality and the absoluteness of the universal sea of unconditioned life. This attitude is emancipating because it removes the imperfect by resolving the mind into the consciousness of the perfect. It produces the realization of the real and thus floods human life with the light of the real, that light that invariably dispels all darkness, whether it be ignorance, adversity, want, weakness, illusion or evil in any form or condition.

The secret of all metaphysical methods of cure is found in the peculiar power of the metaphysical attitude. To enter this attitude is to resolve mind in the consciousness of the absolute, and since there is no sickness in the absolute it is not possible for any mind to feel sickness while in the consciousness of the absolute. For this reason any method that will cause the mind to enter the metaphysical attitude will give that mind the power to heal physical or mental ailments. However, it is not the method that heals. It is that peculiar power or consciousness that conies when the mind is in the metaphysical attitude. And this power simply implies the elimination of imperfect conditions by resolving consciousness into the perfection of absolute states.

The actions of the mind are back of all personal conditions, therefore when the mind begins to act in the consciousness of absolute states it will express the perfection, the health, the wholeness and the power of those states. And when the qualities of such states arc expressed, imperfect conditions must necessarily disappear. Light and darkness cannot exist in the same place at the same time; neither can health and disease. When the former comes the latter is no more. When the mind is placed in the metaphysical attitude the conscious realization of the more powerful forces of life is gained. This means possession and mastery of those forces, at least in a measure, and the result will be a decided increase in the power, the capacity and the ability of every active faculty of the mind.

It is therefore evident that every person who desires to become much and achieve much should live habitually in the metaphysical attitude, for it is in this attitude that the best use of the mind is secured. The metaphysical attitude is distinct from the psychical attitude, and it is highly important for every person to clearly understand this distinction. Both attitudes will place the mind in touch with the more powerful forces of life, but the metaphysical is based upon the conviction that all power is in itself good, and that the mind naturally controls all power ; but the psychical attitude has no definite conviction or purpose regarding the real nature of power. The metaphysical attitude takes hold of those finer powers and applies them constructively, while in the psychical attitude those powers are more or less in a chaotic state. For this reason the psychical attitude is nearly always detrimental, while the metaphysical is never otherwise than highly beneficial.

To approach the universal life of unbounded wisdom and limitless power is usually termed occultism. We find therefore that metaphysics and occultism have the same general purpose, and deal largely with the same elements and powers, but they do not make the same use of those elements and powers, nor are the results identical in any sense whatever. The psychical attitude opens the mind to more power but takes no definite steps in directing that power into constructive channels. If the mind is wholesome and constructive while in the psychical attitude the greater powers thus gained will be beneficial because it will in such a mind be directed properly. But to enter the psychical while there are adverse tendencies, false ideas or perverted desires in mind, is decidedly detrimental because this greater power will at such times be misdirected. And the greater the power the worse will be the consequence when misdirection takes place.

To state it briefly, no mind can safely enter the psychical attitude unless it has a spotless character, a masterful mind, and knows the truth about everything in this present state of existence. But as this requirement is practically beyond everybody, we must conclude that no one can safely enter the psychical state. To enter the psychical attitude is to fill the personality with new forces, some of which will be very strong, and if the mind is not constructive through and through, at the time, some or all of those forces will become destructive.

However, it is not possible to make the mind constructive through and through without entering the metaphysical attitude ; that is, the mind is not fit to enter the psychical attitude until it has entered the metaphysical attitude. But as the same powers are secured in the metaphysical attitude, the psychical attitude becomes superfluous. Therefore, to give a single moment of thought or attention to occultism is a waste of time.

When a mind enters the metaphysical attitude it becomes constructive at once, because the metaphysical attitude is naturally a constructive attitude, being based upon the conviction that all things are in themselves good and working together for greater good. All power is good and all power is constructive. All power is beneficial when applied according to its true purpose, but no mind can apply power according to its true purpose until it becomes thoroughly constructive, and no mind can become thoroughly constructive until it enters the metaphysical attitude.

In this attitude all thought and attention is given to that which makes for better things and greater things. The mind is placed in such perfect harmony with the absolute that it naturally follows the law of the absolute, and to follow this law is to be all that you can be. It is therefore the very soul of advancement, attainment and achievement, having nothing but construction in view.

The fact that the practice of occultism produces extraordinary phenomena, either upon the physical plane or in the world of mental imagery gives it an atmosphere of the marvelous, and therefore it becomes extremely fascinating to the senses. Metaphysics, however, does not aim to appeal directly to the senses nor does it produce mere phenomena. On the contrary, metaphysics appeals directly to the superior understanding, and its purpose is to develop worth, greatness and superiority in man.

Those persons who live habitually in the metaphysical attitude have a wholesome, healthful appearance. They are bright, happy, contented, and they look clean. They are thoroughly alive, but in their expression of life there is a deep calmness that indicates extraordinary power and the high attainment of real harmony. We realize, therefore, why it is only in the metaphysical attitude that we can secure the best use of the mind.

The metaphysical attitude is rich in thoughts and ideas of worth. Such ideas are always constructive, and when applied will invariably promote practical and tangible advancement. To entertain pure metaphysical thought is to grow in the power to create higher thought and also to grow in the conscious realization of the real, thereby eliminating imperfect conditions of mind, thought or personality by resolving the mind in the consciousness of the unconditioned.

Metaphysics deals fundamentally with the understanding of the principle of absolute reality, that is, that complete something that underlies all things, permeates all things and surrounds all things. It deals with the all that there is in the world of fact and reality, and we can readily understand that the mind must aim to deal with the all if its use is to be the best. In other words the best use of the mind naturally implies that use of the mind that gives the highest, the largest and the most comprehensive application of everything there is in the mind. And this the metaphysical attitude invariably tends to do.

The understanding of the principle of absolute reality, that is the soul, so to speak, of all that is real, also reveals the great truth that all individual expressions of life have their source in the perfect state of being, and that the growth of the individual mind in the consciousness of this perfect state of being will cause that same perfection of being to be expressed more and more in the personal man. The term "perfection," however, in this sense implies that state of being that is all that it can be now, and that is so much that nothing in the present state of being can be added.

We all seek perfection, that is, that state where the mind realizes in itself those ideals that are discerned as possibilities within itself; and this form of perfection the metaphysical attitude has the power to produce in any mind at any time. In fact to enter the metaphysical attitude is to give higher and higher degrees of this perfection to every power, every faculty, every function and every talent in human life.

There are various methods for producing the metaphysical attitude, but the better way is to give the first attention to the development of a metaphysical sense; that is, to train the mind to think more and more of that state of consciousness the one predominating factor. When this sense is awakened each mind will find its own best methods. The majority, however, have this sense and need only to place it in action. To give full action to the metaphysical sense we should aim to discern the absolutely real that is within everything of which the mind can be conscious. We should try to carry out this aim in connection with every process of thought, especially those processes that involve the exercise of the imagination.

CHAPTER III.

WHAT DETERMINES MENTAL ACTION.

Every force and faculty in the mind has a tendency to act in a certain way, to move in a certain direction and to produce certain results. It is evident, therefore, that when we control the tendencies of the mind we may determine the actions of the mind and also what results those actions will naturally produce. In addition we may determine whether we are to go forward or backward, towards inferiority or superiority. To control mental tendencies we must control that from which tendencies arise, and all tendencies are born of desires. But desires can be made to order or eliminated, as we may decide.

We are all familiar with the fact that it is not an easy matter to stop "when we get a-going" in any particular direction. For this reason we should direct our movements in the right direction before we begin. And to learn in what direction we are moving we shall only have to examine the tendencies of the mind. When any tendency is established the mind will act unconsciously in that direction and will carry out the desires involved.

In this connection it is highly important to understand that the creative forces in the mind invariably obey and follow tendencies, and always go with those tendencies that have the greatest intensities and the most perfect concentration. When you think that you should like to have this or that you establish a mental tendency to create a desire for that particular thing. And that desire may become uncontrollable, so that, although the tendency comes from a desire that you could control, it may create a desire that you cannot control. Every tendency that is formed in the mind has a tendency to multiply and reproduce itself because an impression is energy centralized, and creative desire always appears with such centralization. When the tendency of an impression to produce itself is permitted that tiny impression may become a powerful mental state and may become so strong that all other states in mind will have to obey. Under such circumstances the man himself will become more and more like that particular state of mind, which fact explains a great many mysteries in human character that have heretofore seemed beyond comprehension.

Some people are exact externalizations of a single predominating mental state while others form their personalities from a group of mental states. But since every mental state originated in some tiny impression, we understand what may become of us when we permit every impression to follow its natural tendency. Every large object, physical or metaphysical, has a tendency to draw all smaller objects into its own path, and also to make all things in its atmosphere like unto itself. This, however, is partly prevented by counteracting tendencies, though the law is an important one and should be thoroughly understood.

In the metaphysical world the understanding of this law is especially important in the building of character and in the development of talents. If you have good character it means that the strongest tendencies of mind are wholesome, elevating and righteous in their nature, while if your character is weak there is not one elevating tendency that is strong enough to predominate in the world of conduct. A perverted character is always the result of descending tendencies with the ascending tendencies too insignificant to exercise and influence.

The fact that weak characters as well as perverted characters sometimes perform noble acts, and that the finest characters sometimes degrade themselves, is readily explained by the law of mental tendencies. In the first case the better tendencies are permitted occasionally to act without interference, while in the second case we find degrading tendencies arising temporarily, possibly through the influence of suggestion. These adverse tendencies, however, could not have exercised any power over conduct had the strong, ascending tendencies been active. But the strongest tendencies may at times be inactive, and it is at these times that a good man may fall, and the other kind show acts of goodness.

When you think more of the external things of life than that which is within, you create in consciousness a tendency to dwell on the surface. The result is you become superficial in proportion and finally become much inferior to what you were. On the other hand, when you think much of those things that are lofty and profound you create in consciousness a tendency to penetrate the deeper things in life. And the result is you become conscious of a larger world of thought, thereby increasing your mental capacity as well as placing yourself in a position where you may make valuable discoveries or formulate ideas of worth.

When you place questionable pictures before minds that are not established in purity, you create in those minds a tendency to immoral desire, and if those tendencies are continued such desires may become too strong to be controlled, and the victims will seek gratification even at the risk of life. This illustrates how powerful a mental tendency may be come and how easily a wrong tendency may be produced when we do not exercise full control over those impressions that may enter the mind.

That man who thinks a great deal about spotless virtue and keeps the idea of virtue constantly before attention will soon create such a strong tendency to virtue that all desires and feelings will actually become virtuous. In consequence it will be simplicity itself for such a person to be virtuous, for when you are virtuous you do not have to try to be. You do not have to resist or fight desires which you do not want because all your desires have become tendencies towards clean and wholesome living. Your energies do not create grosser feelings anymore, but have been trained to create vitality, energy, force and power instead.

Here we should remember that when the predominating tendencies of mind are towards virtue all creative energies will become constructive, and will build up body and mind instead of being dissipated through some desire that is not even normal.

Another illustration of mental tendency and how mental tendency determines mental action is found in the man who is ambitious. Through the efforts of that ambition he is daily training all the tendencies of the mind to act upon the faculties needed to carry out his plans, and he is in consequence building up those faculties with the added force and nourishment thus accumulated. This proves that whenever you resolve to accomplish certain things you will certainly succeed in proportion to your ability. But by resolve we do not mean mere mental spurts. A resolve to be genuine must be constant, and must never waver in the strength of its force and determination. The reason why such a resolve must eventually win is found in the study of mental tendencies; that is, in the realization of the fact that we go as our tendencies go, where we directed them in their first stages.

When we think a great deal about the refined side of life we create tendencies that will cause all the forces within us to recreate everything in our systems according to a more refined pattern. Therefore, to be refined will ere long become second nature, provided we keep constantly before our minds the highest idea of refinement that we can mentally picture. This illustrates how the control of mental tendency may absolutely change an individual from the most ordinary state of grossness to the highest state of refinement.

A striking illustration of the power of mental tendency is found in connection with the belief of the average mind that the body decays and grows old. For this reason we find in practically all human personalities a tendency to produce decay and age in the body. And this tendency is actually bringing about decay and old age where there would be no such conditions whatever were the tendency absent. Nature renews your body every few months and there is no natural process of decay in your system. If your system decays, you yourself have created the process of decay, either through mental or physical violation of natural laws, and by permitting those violations to become permanent tendencies.

If there is a process in your system that makes you look older every year, that process is a false one. It is not placed there by nature. You yourself have produced it by perpetuating the tendency to get older, a tendency that invariably arises from the belief that we must get older. The tendency to become weaker in body and mind as the years go by is also a creation of your own. It is not natural to become weaker with the passing of years. On the contrary, it is natural to become stronger the longer you live, and it is just as easy for you to create a tendency to become stronger the longer you live as it is to create the reverse. In like manner you can also create the tendency to become more attractive in personality, more powerful in mind, stronger in character and more beautiful in soul the longer you live.

However, we must eliminate all detrimental tendencies of the mind, and to do so we must find their origin. In many instances we are born with these adverse tendencies although many of them are acquired later in life. Those tendencies with which we are born generally become stronger and stronger through our own tendency to follow the groove in which we are placed. We find, therefore, that it is always a mistake to live in a groove or to continue year after year to do a certain thing in the same usual way. Our object should be to break bounds constantly and to improve upon everything. Nothing is more important than change, provided every change is a constructive change.

Every impression that we form in the mind is a seed which may grow a tendency. Therefore we should not only eliminate all such impressions as we refuse to cultivate, but we should also prevent inferior and perverse impressions from entering the mind in the first place. To do this, however, we must be constantly on watch so that nothing can enter the mind through our senses which we do not wish to possess and perpetuate.

When we see people growing old, or rather becoming old through the operation of certain false tendencies, the impression of an aging process will stamp itself upon our minds if we permit it. Such impressions contain the tendency to produce the same aging process in us and it usually receives our permission to have its way. Thus we cause the aging process to become stronger and stronger in us the more we see it in others until we soon discover that we are actually creating for ourselves older bodies every year. The new bodies that nature gives us every year are thus made to look older than the new bodies of the year before, which is a direct violation of natural law. Then we also sing with much feeling about the death and decay that is everywhere about us, and entertain thoughts of a similar nature by the wholesale. But all these indications of death and decay in our environments were not produced by nature. They were produced by false mental tendencies which arose through false belief about life and human nature.

The same is true regarding all other adverse tendencies that may exist in us or in those with whom we associate. When we see the action of those tendencies in others we receive impressions upon our own minds that have it in them to produce the same tendencies in us, which will later bring about the same adverse consequences in us. Therefore we must not permit our minds to be impressed with anything in our environment that is contrary to what is true in the perfect nature of man. In other words, we must never permit any mental impression that comes from the weak, the adverse or the wrong conditions about us, but we should permit all things that are good and constructive to impress our minds more and more deeply every day.

We have been in the habit of thinking that various things were natural and inevitable because we 'see them everywhere about us, but when we discover that we have made a great many of these things ourselves and that they are all wrong, and that it is just as easy to make them different, we conclude that it is time to begin all over again. But to begin, we must transform all the tendencies of the mind so that all of them will move in the way we wish to go.

We may wish to enter health, but if there are tendencies to disease in our systems, and especially in the subconscious, our physical bodies will evolve more or less disease every year. Therefore this tendency must be changed to one of health before we can have what we desire in this respect. In other words, every action in the human system must be a health producing action and such will be the case when all the tendencies of the system have perfect health as their goal. The same is true regarding all other desires, tendencies or objects we may have in view.

The first question, therefore, to ask is this: Where am I going? Or rather, Where are the tendencies of my mind going? Are those tendencies moving towards sin, sickness, decay, weakness and failure, or are they moving towards the reverse? We must look at ourselves closely and learn whether those tendencies are moving where we wish to go, or moving towards conditions that we know to be wrong or detrimental. And when we find where these tendencies are moving we must proceed to change them if they are wrong, and this we can do by producing right mental tendencies in their stead.

When we look at the tendencies of our mind we can largely determine what our own future is to be, provided we do not change those tendencies later on. Then when we know that our present physical conditions, our present strength, our present ability, our present character, our present attainments and our present achievements are all the consequences of the way our mental tendencies have been moving, and also that we have lived, thought and acted according to those tendencies when we know these things, we shall have found knowledge of priceless value, and by applying that knowledge we can make our own future as we wish it to be.

The question is, whither are we drifting, not physically but mentally, because it is the way we drift mentally that determines both the actions of the mind and the actions of the body. And our mental tendencies answer this question. As they go so do we go. What we are creating, what we are building, what we are developing these things depend upon how the tendencies of the mind are directed. Therefore the proper course to pursue is to determine where we wish to go, in what direction and when. Then establish in mind what we wish to accomplish and how soon.

Know what you want and what you want to be. Then examine all the tendencies of your mind. All those which are not going the way you want to go must be changed, while all those that are already going your way should be given more and more power. Then do not waver in your purpose. Never look back, let nothing disturb your plans, and keep your highest aspirations too sacred to be mentioned. You will find that if you will pursue this course you will go where you wish to go, you will achieve what you have planned, and your destiny will be as you desire.

CHAPTER IV.

THE LEADING METAPHYSICAL LAW.

Whatever enters the consciousness of man will express itself in the personality of man. This is one of the most important of all the laws of life, and when its immense scope is fully comprehended thousands of perplexing questions will be answered. We shall then know why we are as we are and why all things about us are as they are ; and we shall also know how all this can be changed. When we examine the principle upon which this law is based we find that our environments are the results of our actions and our actions are the results of our thoughts. Our physical and mental conditions are the results of our states of mind and our states of mind are the results of our ideas. Our thoughts are mental creations patterned after the impressions that exist in consciousness and our ideas are the mental conceptions that come from our conscious understanding of life. Thus we realize that everything existing both in the mental field and in the personality, as well as in surrounding conditions, have their origin in that which becomes active in human consciousness.

We may define consciousness by stating that it is an attribute of the Ego through which the individual knows what is and what is taking place. Consciousness may usually be divided into three phases, the objective, the subjective and the absolute. Through absolute consciousness the Ego discerns its relationship with the universal that phase of consciousness that is beyond the average mind and need not necessarily be considered in connection with this law. Through subjective consciousness the Ego knows what is taking place within itself, that is, within the vast field of individuality. And through objective consciousness the Ego knows what is taking place in its immediate external world. Objective consciousness employs the five external senses, while subjective consciousness employs all those finer perceptions which, when grouped together are sometimes spoken of as the sixth sense.

In our study of this law we shall deal principally with subjective consciousness because it is this consciousness that rules over real interior action. The subjective plane is the plane of change and growth so that there can be no change in any part of life until the cause of the desired change has been found or produced in the subjective. What enters objective consciousness will not produce any effect upon the personality unless it also enters subjective consciousness, because it is only what becomes subjective that reproduces itself in the human entity.

In our present state of existence the center of conscious action is largely in the subconscious mind, that is, the interior or finer mental field, and in consequence all the actions of consciousness are directly connected with the subjective. In this connection it is well to state that the terms subjective and subconscious mean practically the same. Whatever enters consciousness and is deeply felt will impress itself upon the subjective so therefore in order to control the results of this law we must avoid giving deep feelings to such impressions, thoughts, ideas or desires as we do not wish to have reproduced in ourselves. There are many impressions and experiences that enter objective consciousness to a degree, but never become subjective since they are not accompanied with depth of feeling. We may be conscious of such experiences or impressions, but we are not affected by them. For this reason we need not give them our attention, which is well because the majority of the impressions that enter the conscious mind pass off, so to speak, without affecting life in any way.

Whatever actually enters consciousness is always felt by the finer sensibilities of mind, and whatever enters into the finer state of mind is taken up by the creative energies; and impressions are accordingly produced. From these impressions will come similar expressions, and it is such expressions that determine thought, character, conduct and life. To state this law in a slightly different manner we may state that whatever enters subjective consciousness will produce an impression just like itself, and every subjective impression becomes a pattern for thought creation while it lasts. Therefore when ever an impression is formed in the mind, thoughts will be created just like that impression. And so long as that impression remains in subjective consciousness thought will continue to be formed after its likeness. Then we must remember that every thought created in the mind goes out into the personality, producing vital and chemical effects according to its nature.

Thus we understand the process of the law. First, the impression is formed upon subjective consciousness. Second, the creative energies of the mind will produce thoughts and mental states just like those impressions, and all such thoughts and mental states will express themselves in the personality, producing conditions in the personality similar to their own nature. To illustrate this process from everyday life we may mention several experiences with which we are all familiar.

When you view a very peaceful scene and become wholly absorbed in it your entire being will become perfectly serene almost at once, and this is the reason : The scene was peaceful and produced a peaceful impression upon your mind. This impression entered your subjective consciousness because you became deeply absorbed in the scene. If you had simply viewed the scene in a superficial way you would have felt no change because then the impression would not have entered your subjective mind; but you responded to the impressions that entered the mind through the organ of sight and thus admitted those impressions into the deeper or subjective state. In other words, the scene actually entered into your consciousness, the serenity of it all was impressed upon the subjective; and as explained in the process above, the creative energies of your mind at once began to create thoughts and mental states containing the same serene and peaceful life. These thoughts entered into your entire personality, as all thoughts do after being created, thus conveying the life of peace to every atom in your being.

When you view an exciting scene and are carried away by it you lose your poise and may even become uncontrollable. The reason is you admit confusion into your mind, and according to the law, confusion will be produced in yourself ; that is, discord has entered your consciousness and has be- come the model for the creative processes of the mind. The mental energies will enter such states and create thoughts and mental states that are just AS confused as the confusion you saw in the without. And when these confused states go out into the personality, as they do almost at once, your entire nervous system will be upset, disturbed and in a state of inharmony. Thus you have produced the same confusion in your own mind and body that you saw in your environments. However, if you had prevented the confused scenes from entering your mind, you would have been perfectly calm in the midst of it all; but by permitting the excitement to enter your consciousness it was reproduced in yourself, and the discord that entered your consciousness from the without was thereby expressed in your own personality. There may be indications of threatening failure in your work and you may begin to fear that such failure will come, but so long as you do not feel the inner dread of failure the impression of failure will not enter your consciousness ; and accordingly conditions of failure will not be produced in your own mind. But if the fear continues until you actually feel fearful deep down in your heart, the idea of failure has entered your consciousness, and if not prevented will be deeply impressed in the subjective.

When failure is impressed upon your subjective mind, a condition of mental failure will permeate all your faculties, and in consequence they will fail to do their best. And we all know very well that the very moment our faculties begin to go back on us, doing less work and less effective work, we are on the down grade to failure and loss. Failure means going down to the lesser, and if you have admitted thoughts of failure into your mind you have given your creative energies bad models. These energies will create thoughts and mental states just like those models, no matter what those models may be. If those models are based upon the idea of failure all the thoughts created will contain the failing attitude, or the losing ground attitude. When such thoughts express themselves in the system they will produce weaking conditions and disturbances everywhere in mind and personality. Your faculties will not be able to do their best ; they will begin to fail in their work because they are being permeated with a losing ground tendency, and you will make many mistakes on account of the increasing confusion. The result will be inevitable failure unless you are able to check this tendency or retrace your steps upward before it is too late. We have all noticed that the man on the down grade makes more mistakes than anyone else, and also that his genius or his talents become weaker the further down he goes. The above explains the reason why.

We are all familiar with the folly of judging from appearances and permitting temporary conditions to impress and govern our thinking, the reason being that our object is not to follow the whims of circumstances or the uncertainties of fate, but to carry out our purpose in life regardless of what happens. On the other hand when we do not judge according to external indications, but proceed to impress the subconscious mind with the determination to succeed, we are placing in consciousness an idea that stands for growth, advancement and increase. Immediately the creative energies of mind will proceed to create thoughts and states that have advancing, upbuilding and constructive tendencies. Such thoughts will give push, power, life and added talent to your faculties, and you will very soon begin to do better work; the superior forces will build up your mind, make your mind more brilliant, and add constantly to your capacity.

Thus you will become a success within yourself ; that is, your own forces and faculties will begin to work successfully which is the first essential to the gaining of success in the external world. You will be moving forward in your own being and you will be gaining in worth in every respect. The results will be better work, better impressions upon the world, and fewer mistakes. And when the world discovers that there is success in you they will want your service with recompense according to your full worth. When we understand this process of the mind we realize how we can bring upon our selves almost anything simply through permitting the corresponding impressions to enter consciousness. Therefore we should learn to prevent all such things from entering consciousness as we do not wish to see reproduced in ourselves and expressed through our personality. Then we should learn to impress permanently in consciousness the image and likeness of all those things that we do wish to develop and express.

The workings of this law are very well illustrated in conditions of heath and disease, because when we are constantly thinking about disease and fearing disease we permit the idea of disease to impress itself upon consciousness. In other words, we become more and more conscious of disease, and cause the image of sickness to get a firm foothold in the subjective. The result is that the creative forces of mind will create thoughts, mental states and conditions just like the image of disease, and that which is just like the image of disease actually is a disease. Therefore since every mental state conveys conditions similar to itself to every part of the body, such thoughts will constantly carry diseased conditions into the body, tending thereby to produce the very ailment that we feared, thought of, or impressed upon consciousness in the first place. Nature may resist these adverse conditions for a while if the body is full of vitality, but when the vital forces run low these sickly mental conditions will have full sway, and the result will be a siege of illness which may be prolonged, and even result in death, which happens thousands of times under just such conditions.

The law, however, works both ways. We can just as easily impress the idea of perfect health upon subjective consciousness and thus give the creative forces a better image as a model for their creative processes. At such times all thoughts and mental states will be wholesome and health producing, and will constantly carry better health, more harmony and greater strength to the body. This is how the law works, and as anyone can understand the process, further details are not required. Briefly stated, the law is this: That everything entering subjective consciousness will impress itself there and become a pattern for the creative energies of the mind. These energies will proceed to create thoughts and conditions just like the impression formed, which will carry their own conditions to every part of the human system.

In this way conditions are produced and expressed in the personality just like the original idea, thought or impression that entered subjective consciousness. Everything that enters the mind through the various senses may also enter subjective consciousness, that is, if deeply felt, and thus produce a permanent impression. In like manner, all our own concepts of things will become impressions, that is, if they are inner convictions. For this reason we must not only watch all those things that enter the mind through the senses, but we must also govern our own thinking so that every mental conception formed will be one of quality, worth, wholeness, health, growth and advancement.

To employ this law properly nothing must be permitted to enter the subjective unless we wish to have it reproduced in ourselves. We should refuse therefore to take into consciousness that which we do not wish to see expressed through mind or body. We should train consciousness to respond only to those external impressions that are desirable; and we should train our own imaging faculties to impress deeply and permanently in consciousness every good thing or desirable quality that we wish to see reproduced in ourselves and expressed through our personality.

CHAPTER V.

HOW THE MIND MAKES THE MAN.

Man gradually grows into the likeness of that which he thinks of the most. This is another important metaphysical law, and is so closely related to the law presented in the preceding chapter that the analysis given for one will naturally explain the process of the other. However, this second law is distinct from the first one in many of its phases, and it is so full of possibility that the understanding of its application opens up a vast world of change and attainment along a number of lines.

Man is the reflection of all his thought; that is, his body, his. character, his mind, his spiritual nature all are fashioned according to his thought; even the elements that compose the flesh of his body are gross or fine just as his thought happens to be. Whenever we think a great deal of the material, most of our thoughts will become material in their nature and will carry material conditions to every part of the system. This explains why gross thoughts stamp grossness upon every fiber of the body, while refined thought refines every fiber, improving the quality and perfecting the structure.

The mind that thinks a great deal of the perfection of the Supreme will think a great deal of divine qualities and spiritual attainments. In brief, nearly all the thought created in such a mind will be of a superior nature and will carry superiority to every part of the system. When we think more of the spiritual than we do of other things the entire system will constantly pass through a refining and spiritualizing process, the possibility of which if carried on to the ultimate would be nothing less than marvelous. When we think a great deal of power, ability and attainment we are actually creating a great deal of ability in us. We are increasing our power and we are moving forward into far greater attainments.

The mind that thinks constantly of perfect health refusing to entertain for a moment the thought of disease is steadily growing into a state of health that will ere long be absolutely perfect. Such a person may be suffering from a score of maladies now, but all of them must pass away before the constant influx of health, wholeness and life. All darkness must finally vanish from a place that is constantly being filled with more and more light. In like manner any condition that may exist in the person of man will have to change and improve if the person is constantly being filled with a superior condition.

We become like the thoughts we think because the creative power of thought is the only creative power that we have within us. And the energies of mind are constantly creating; and what they create now is just like the thoughts we think now. Since every physical condition, every mental state, and every phase of character since all these things are fashioned after our predominating thoughts, and since the capacity of every faculty and the quality of every talent are determined by the thoughts we think, we must naturally conclude that there can be no greater art than the art of correct thinking. In fact, to think is to occupy a position involving far greater responsibility than that of a thousand absolute monarchs. And when we realize this, we will not permit a single thought to take shape and form in our minds without first determining upon the value of that thought.

Why we grow into the likeness of that of which we think the most has been fully explained in the preceding chapter, and it is found in the fact that every impression formed in the mind will reproduce its kind and express its creations throughout the entire system. And though these impressions usually come from without in the first place, still they do not become real impressions until we accept them into our consciousness, or in thought, or in conviction. That is, many minds will think only what is suggested to them by environment, or what they are told to think by those in authority; still it is their own thought that shapes their lives. Wherever the suggestion may come from, it is your thought about that suggestion that produces the effect.

The analysis of thought presented in the preceding chapter explains how the person is affected by thought, and how thought is always created in the likeness of those ideas, states or impressions that have established themselves in consciousness. But to carry this analysis to its final goal we must discover why man becomes like his thought and also how he can think thought of a superior nature. And this we discover through the workings of the law now under consideration. In the first place man becomes like his thought because there is no other pattern in his being besides his own thought. The creative forces of his mind and personality always create according to the image and likeness of the strongest and deepest impressions in consciousness, and all such impressions are produced by the process of thinking.

When we use the term "thought," however, we may refer either to the mental model, which is the result of mental conception, or we may refer to that thought which is the result of mental creation. The mental creation is patterned after the mental conception, and the mental conception is the result of our efforts to understand what we are thinking about. Mental conception is conscious and is therefore under our control, while mental creation is subconscious and is therefore beyond our control; but we do not have to control mental creation. Those creations will be just like our mental conceptions; therefore when we form only such mental conceptions as we like we shall have only such mental creations as we like. In consequence when we see mentally that which is superior and can form a true conception of what we see, we give to the creative energies a model that is higher than any we have given them before. Accordingly the mental creations will be superior.

And here we should remember that these creations are not wholly abstract, but are in most instances as concrete or tangible as the body itself. The creative energies of the human system act both in the mind and in the body, though their central field of action is always in the subjective or inner side of things. In the body these energies constitute the vital forces and the nerve forces of the system, while in the mind they constitute all those energies or powers employed in thought, feeling or mental action of whatever nature.

When we examine these energies we find that they do not simply create conditions after the likeness of the predominating thought, but that they themselves also become just like the predominating thought, which fact illustrates the power exercised by such thoughts as hold the ruling position in our minds. From this fact we conclude that these forces will give vitality to the body that corresponds to the states of the mind. So, that if there is anything wrong in the subjective states of the mind these forces will convey those wrong conditions to the body, the reason being that these forces come from the subjective and cannot be different from the ruling conditions of their source.

The fibers and cells of the body are built up by these energies. Therefore the quality as well as the structures of the cells must correspond with the nature of the creative energies at the time. These energies build cells just like the patterns before them, and the patterns are formed by the subjective conceptions. When that part of the subjective mind that governs cell structures in the body becomes imbued with a more perfect idea of construction the creative energies will build more perfect cells. And when that part of the subjective mind that governs physical shape and form receives a better conception of shape and form, these creative energies will naturally build a body that is more perfect as to shape and form. Every function in the body is governed by a certain part of the subjective mind and the creative energies act through that particular function according to the present state of the subjective mind.

Therefore when more perfect patterns are placed in .those parts of the subjective that govern the body, the creative energies will build a more perfect body. And when we know that these creative energies are building us a new body every year, according to the predominating pattern of the subjective, we can see how easily the new body we receive every year can be made more perfect if we will improve the subjective pattern. The creative energies construct brain cells in the same way, the quality being governed by the state of mind. And that part of the brain that is to receive the largest group of cells is determined by the tendencies of the mind.

In the world of talents and faculties the creative energies construct concepts so that every talent is actually composed of all the conceptions that the mind has formed while trying to understand the nature and possibility of that talent. In the formation of character the creative energies do their work in constructing desires, motives, purposes and the like. And in every instance they form these characteristics according to the predominating thought on the subject. In the construction of the spiritual attitudes and higher attainments the process is very similar though in these instances the pattern is gained through faith instead of subjective mentation.

Why man grows into the likeness of that which he thinks of the most becomes perfectly clear when we understand how the creative energies work; that is, that they always create after the likeness of the subjective pattern. And when we learn that the subjective pattern can be changed in any part of mind by thinking a great deal of a higher conception of that particular phase, we have the whole secret. When we think a great deal along any line with a higher conception before us we finally establish that higher conception in the place of the old one. When we hold an idea in mind a long time that idea will become a predominating idea; it will become larger and stronger than the other ideas and will consequently be selected as a model by the creative energies.

The next question before us is how to think only of those things that we desire to grow into the likeness of. And this question is answered through the following metaphysical law: Man thinks the most both consciously and unconsciously of that which he loves the best. The simplest way to govern thought is to do so through love. When we love the lofty and the noble we naturally think a great deal of those qualities without trying to do so, and in consequence we become more noble in thought, character and motives. If we wish to develop the greater and the higher within us we must love everything that contains greatness, and our love must be with the whole heart: that is, every fiber of our being must actually thrill with a passion for that higher something which we desire to develop.

Here we must remember that all intellectual or metaphysical methods for the development of talents or character, or anything of a superior nature within us, will fail unless we passionately love superior attainments. The man who loves honesty, justice and virtue will become honest, just and virtuous; though if he does not naturally love those things no amount of moral training can change his character. Millions of people are praying to become better, more noble and more spiritual, but too many fail to receive answers to such prayers. And the reason why is found in the fact that they do not love as deeply as they should those superior attainments for which they are praying. They may desire those things in a superficial way, but that is not sufficient. Real love alone will avail because such love goes to the very depth of life and touches the very essence of being itself.

When we, as a race, will begin to love the superior and the divine with the same depth that we love gold or material pleasures, we shall become a superior race. When we love divine qualities with the whole heart we shall think a great deal of such qualities and the more we will try to understand the inner nature of those qualities. The higher this understanding becomes the higher will our conception of the divine and the spiritual become. And the higher those conceptions are the higher

will be our thoughts. And since the outer man is fashioned after the ruling thoughts of his mind, we shall in this way steadily rise in the scale of life until we become in mind and personality like those higher thoughts we have learned to think. In other words, we shall manifest in the without more and more of the divinity that is within. And that such a process would in time transform humanity into a superior race anyone can readily understand.

Love, however, is not mere sentiment, nor is it ordinary emotionalism. Love also has quality. There is ordinary love and there are the higher forms of quality. Therefore, the love with which we love must be developed into greater worth if we are to penetrate the realms of worth through our love. The reason why we naturally think the most about what we like the best is found in the fact that there can be no division in love. When you actually love something that something will receive your undivided attention. And as all your thought goes where your attention is directed you will in this manner give all your thought both consciously and unconsciously to that which you love. This we all know from our own personal experience, and we shall find that everybody has had the same experience, thus proving universally the absoluteness of this law.

We have all seen people become beautiful in countenance and character after they had begun to love some high and noble purpose. And we can find thousands who have become more and more common because they have continued to love the ordinary. By living the ordinary they naturally became like the ordinary thus their mental actions became inferior, and both mind and personality became inferior in proportion. The elements of the body may be in a low state of action and express grossness, or they may be in a high state of action and express refinement; and the state of the mind determines what those actions are to be, whether they are to be crude or refined. The low, common mind invariably gives sluggish or crude actions to the system, and in such a person the physical form looks very much like ordinary clay. But a lofty mind, a mind that is living in the ideal and the beautiful, and in the realization of the marvelous possibilities of mind, gives highly refined actions to the body; and such a body will naturally be superior in fineness, quality and substance. It is therefore true that there are people who are made of a finer clay; not because they have come from so-called noble ' ancestors, but because their thoughts have become beautiful, lofty and high.

The attitude of love towards all that is superior should be cultivated with the greatest enthusiasm, and the love itself should also be made superior as we advance in the realization of true worth. It is in this way that we shall find the true path and the simple path to high thinking, noble thinking and right thinking. And man grows into the likeness, steadily and surely, of that which he thinks of the most.

Since we think the most of what we love the best we should love passionately all that is beautiful and sublime; we should love all that is lofty and ideal; we should love the true side, the superior side and the genuine side in all persons and in all things. But we should never think of the inferior at any time. We should love the perfect, the divine and the spiritual in every soul in existence, and give the whole heart to the love of the sublime qualities of the Supreme. Thus we shall find that body, mind and soul will respond to the perfect thought that we thus form while living on the mental heights. Gradually we shall find all the elements of our nature changing for the better, becoming more and more like those sublime states of mind of which we are so vividly conscious while on the heights.

CHAPTER VI.

HOW MENTAL PICTURES BECOME REALITIES.

Every thought is patterned after the mental image that predominates at the time the thought is created. This is another great metaphysical law and its importance is found in the fact that thought are things, that every thought produces an effect on mind and body, and that the effect is always similar to the cause. According to these facts we can therefore produce any effect desired upon mind or body by producing the necessary thought or mental state, so that when we have learned to control our thinking we can control practically everything else in life, because in the last analysis it is thinking that constitutes the one great cause in the life of the individual.

To control thinking, however, we must understand the process of thought creation. To think is to create thought, and to control thinking is to create any thought we like at any time and under any circumstance. When we analyze the process of thinking we find three factors involved ; that is, the pattern, the mental substance and the creative energy. The pattern is always the deepest impression, the clearest image, or the predominating idea. The quality of the mental substance improves with the quality of the mind; and the quantity increases with the expansion of consciousness, while the creative energies grow stronger the less energy we lose and the more we awaken the greater powers from within.

When an idea or image is impressed upon the mind the mental energies will proceed to create thought just like that image ; and will continue while that image occupies a permanent position in consciousness. When the mind is very active a great deal of thought is created every second, though the amount varies with the activity of the mind. It is therefore more detrimental for an active mind to think wrong thought than for a mind that is dull or stupid; proving the fact that responsibility always increases as we rise in the scale. It is the function of the creative energies of the mind to create thought that is just like every image impressed upon mind and to continue to create thought in the likeness of that image while it lasts. The creative energies do this of their own accord and we cannot stop them. But we can make them weak or strong, or give them better patterns.

Mind is an art gallery of many pictures, but only the most prominent are selected for models in thought creation. Only those pictures that are sufficiently distinct to be seen by consciousness without special effort are brought before the creative energies as patterns. We thus find that the art of controlling one's thinking and the power to determine what kind of thought is to be created is acquired largely through the training of the mind to impress deeply only such mental pictures as are desired as models for thinking. The law, however, is very simple because as the picture in the mind happens to be at this moment so will also be the thoughts created at this moment, and the mental pictures are in each case the ideas and impressions that we permit in mind.

Whatever enters the mind through the senses can impress the mind, and the result will be a picture or mental image which will become a pattern for the creative energies. What takes shape and form in your mind through your own interior thinking will also impress the mind and become an image or pattern. It is therefore possible through this law to determine what kind of thoughts you are to create by impressing your mind with your own ideas regardless of what environment may suggest to you through your senses. And it is by exercising this power that you place the destiny of body, mind and soul absolutely in your own hands.

As we proceed with this process we find another vital law which may be stated as follows : What we constantly picture upon the mind we shall eventually realize in actual life. This law may be spoken of as a twin sister to the one stated above as they are found to work together in almost every process of thought creation and thought expression. The one declares that all thought is patterned after the predominating mental pictures while the other declares that the entire external life of man is being daily recreated in the likeness of those mental pictures. The fact is, as the mental tendencies are, so is thought; as thought is, so is character; and it is the combined action of character, ability and purpose that determines what we are to attain or accomplish, or what is to happen to us.

Through the law of attraction we naturally meet in the external world what corresponds to our own internal world, that is, to what we are in ourselves. The self constitutes the magnet, and like attracts like. This self which constitutes the magnet is composed of all the active forces, desires, tendencies, motives, states and thoughts that are at work in mind or personality. When we look at everything that is alive throughout our whole being and put all those things together we have what may be termed our present active self. And this self invariably attracts in the external world such conditions as correspond to its own nature. This self and all its parts in the person corresponds to the thoughts that we have been creating in mind. In fact the nature of the self is actually composed of thought, mental states and mental activities. We realize, therefore, that when we change our thought, the nature of the self will change, and this change will be good or otherwise depending upon the change of thought.

Your external life is the exact counterpart of this active self. This self is the exact likeness of your thought, and your thoughts are patterned after the pictures that are impressed upon your mind. Therefore we understand that whatever is pictured in the mind will be realized in external life. And the reason why is not only simply explained but can be proven along strictly scientific lines. However, to determine through the law of mind picturing what our external life is to be, every process of mind picturing which we desire to carry out must be continued for a sufficient length of time to give the creative processes the opportunity to make over the whole self.

When a certain picture is formed in the mind thought will be created in the likeness of that picture. This thought goes out and permeates the entire self and changes the self to a degree. But as a rule it takes some time to change the entire self ; therefore we must continue to hold the desired picture in mind until the whole self has been entirely made over and has become just like the ideal picture. And you can easily discern when the self has been wholly changed because as soon as the self is changed everything in your life changes. Then a new self will attract new people, new conditions, new environments, new opportunities and new states of being. It is evident therefore that so long as there is no change in the outer life we may know that the self has not been changed. However, the changing process may be going on, but the new has not as yet become stronger than the old, and for the time being things continue as they were.

When the self has been changed to such an extent that the new becomes positive and the old negative we will begin to attract new things. We may therefore begin to attract new and better things for some time before the entire self has been completely changed. When we are changing only a part of the self that part will begin to attract the new while those parts of the self that have not been changed will continue to attract the old as usual. This explains why some people continue to attract trouble and adversity for a while after they have begun to live a larger and a better life.

In promoting the art of mind picturing we must not change ideas or plans at too frequent intervals for such changes will neutralize what has been gained thus far and here is the place where a great many people fail. The average person who wishes to change his life for the better does not hold on to his ideals long enough; that is, he does not give them a fair chance to work themselves out and bring the expected results. When he does not receive results as soon as he expects he changes his plans and produces new pictures upon the mind. Thus he begins all over again, losing what he had built up through previous plans; but ere long becomes discouraged once more, so tries still other ideas or methods. When our ideals are the highest we know we do not have to change them. They cannot be improved upon until we have so entirely recreated ourselves that we can live in a superior state of consciousness. It is therefore highly important to determine positively upon the ideals that we wish to realize, and to hold on to those ideals until they are realized regardless of what may happen in the meantime.

However, we must not infer that we can realize in the external the correspondence of every picture that we hold in mind, because the majority of the mental pictures that we form are so constituted that they can be worked out in practical action. We must therefore distinguish between such ideals as can be made practical now and those that are simply temporary dreams, having no connection with real life here and now.

To be realized a mental picture must be constant, but only such pictures can be constant as are sufficiently elaborate to involve a complete transformation in yourself, and that are so high that they can act as an inspiration until all your present ideals are realized. When we form such pictures in the mind and continue to hold on to them until they are externally realized we shall certainly obtain the desired realization. At such times we can proceed with the perfect faith that what we have pictured will become true in actual life in days to come, and those days will not be far away. But to use this law the mind must never waver; it must hitch its wagon to a star and never cut the traces.

In scientific mind picturing it is not necessary to go into minor details, though we must not be too general. The idea is to picture all the essentials, that is, all those parts that are distinct or individualized. But we need not include such things as are naturally attracted by the essentials. In other words, apply the law, and that which will naturally come through the application of that law, will be realized.

If you wish to realize a more perfect body it is not necessary to picture the exact physical appearance of that body. You may not know at present what a perfect body should look like. Therefore picture only the quality of perfection in every part of the physical form and those qualities will develop and express themselves more and more throughout your personality. And if you wish to enter a different environment do not give your thought to some special locality, nor to persons and things that would necessarily be included in such an environment. Persons come and go and things are generally the way we wish them to be.

To proceed realize what constitutes an ideal environment and hold that picture in your mind. In analyzing an ideal environment we would find it to contain harmony, beauty, love, peace, joy, desirable opportunities, advantages, ideal friends, wholesome conditions and an abundance of the best of every thing that the welfare of human life may require. Therefore we should picture those things and continue to hold them in mind with the faith that we will soon find an environment containing all those things in the highest degree of perfection. Gradually we shall find more and more of them coming into our life until we shall find an environment that comes up in every respect to our ideal.

The law of mind picturing will also be found effective in changing physical conditions. Any physical malady must eventually disappear if we continue to hold in mind a perfect picture of health and wholeness. Many have eliminated chronic ailments in a few weeks and even in a few days by this method, and all would succeed if they never pictured disease but perfect health only. In the field of achievement we will find the same facts to hold good. Whenever we fear that we shall not succeed we bring forth the wrong picture thus the wrong thoughts are created and wrong conditions are produced; in consequence the very thing we feared comes upon us. When we are positively determined to succeed, however, we picture the idea of success and attainment upon the mind, and according to the law, success will be realized in external life.

Mental and spiritual attainments respond remarkably to mind picturing, principally because all true mind picturing draws consciousness up into the world of superiority. The same is true in the field of talent. If there is any talent that you wish to develop draw mental pictures of yourself in full possession of that talent and you will comply with the requirements of the steady growth of that talent. This method alone will accomplish much, but when it is associated with our processes of development the results desired will surely be remarkable.

In the building of character, mind picturing is of exceptional importance. If you continue to associate only with impure minds and continue to think only of deeds of darkness you will picture only the wrong upon your mind. Thus your thoughts will become wrong and wrong thoughts lead to wrong actions. The contrary, however, is also true. So therefore if we wish to perfect our conduct we must impress upon the mind only such ideas as will inspire us with desires and aims for greater and higher things.

We all admit that character can be influenced most decidedly by mind pictures, but everybody may not be ready to accept the idea that ability, attainment, achievement, environment and destiny can be affected in the same way. However, it is only a full analysis of the law of mind picturing that is necessary to prove this also to be an exact scientific fact. It is the way we think that determines the quality of the mind, and it is the quality of the mind that determines what our ability, mental capacity and mental force is to be. And we can readily understand that the improvement of ability will naturally be followed by increase in attainment and achievement as well as a greater control over fate and destiny.

Man is constantly increasing his ability, is making his own future and is making that future brighter and greater every day. Therefore, if mind pictures can affect mental quality, mental power and mental ability they can also affect environment and achievement, and in brief, the entire external life of man. In looking for evidence for the fact that mental pictures can affect ability, simply compare results from efforts that are inspired by high ideals and efforts that are inspired by low ideals, and you have all the evidence you need.

When your mind is filled with pictures of superiority you will think superior thoughts thoughts that have more quality, power and worth, and such thoughts cannot fail to give power, quality and worth to your talents and faculties. We also find that tendencies, desires and motives originate largely from mental pictures, and we also know that these factors exercise an enormous power in life. The active self of man is so dominated by desires and tendencies that it is absolutely impossible to change the self until tendencies and desires are changed. But tendencies and desires as well as motives cannot be changed without changing the mental pictures a fact of extreme importance.

Through scientific mind picturing you can create or eliminate any kind of desire ; you can produce or remove any tendency that you like. All that is necessary is to impress upon the mind the perfect picture of a desire or tendency that you wish and then continue to hold that picture in the mind until you have results. A mental picture, however, is not necessarily something that you can see in the same way as you see external, tangible things. It is an impression or idea or concept and is seen only by the understanding. In order to hold a mental picture constantly in mind keep all the essentials of that picture before your attention ; that is, try to be conscious of the real nature of those powers and possibilities that are represented by the picture. In other words, enter into the very nature of those qualities which that picture represents.

The mind is very large. It is therefore possible to form mental pictures of as many ideals as we like, but at first it is best to choose only a few. Begin by picturing a perfect body, an able mind a strong character and a beautiful soul ; after that an ideal interior life and an ideal external environment. Thus you have the foundation of a great life, a rich life and a wonderful life. Keep these pictures constantly before your mind in fact, train yourself to actually live for those pictures. And you will find all things in your life changing daily to become more and more like those pictures. In the course of time you will realize in actual life the exact likeness of those pictures; that is, what you have constantly pictured upon your mind you will realize in actual life. Then you can form new and more beautiful pictures to be realized in like manner as you build for a still greater future.

CHAPTER VII.

THE INCREASE OF MENTAL POWER.

All mental actions that consciously move towards the within tend to increase the capacity, the power and the quality of mind. The majority of mental actions in the average mind, however, move towards the surface, and this is one reason why advancing years bring mental inferiority as the converse of this law is also true. That is, that all mental actions that move towards the surface will decrease the power of mind.

According to the law of growth the more we use a faculty the larger and stronger and more perfect it should become, provided it is used properly. Therefore continuous use in itself should invariably bring increase. However, the use of anything may follow the lines of destruction as well as construction. For this reason we must train all mental actions along constructive lines. And we find all constructive action tends to deepen mental action; in other words, tends to move towards the within.

The value of the increase of mental power is clearly evident along all lines. Everything must increase in the life of him who is perpetually increasing his own personal power. We know that a large mind creates more extensively than a small one. The creations of a highly developed mind are more worthy than the creations of an inferior mind, and the achievements of any one are in proportion to that one's capacity and power. Therefore when we begin to increase the value of life everything pertaining to life as well as everything coming into life will increase also. Perpetual development in ourselves means perpetual increase of everything of worth required in our sphere of existence. This is the law; but so long as mental actions move towards the surface, mentality is diminished; therefore the opposite process must be established.

By training all mental actions to move constantly towards the within we increase perpetually the capacity, the power and the quality of mind and the reason why is very simple. When mental actions move towards the surface consciousness will be centered upon the surface of things and will therefore picture in mind the lesser and inferior side of things. Those mental energies that serve as patterns for the creative energies will in consequence be formed in the likeness of the smaller. And the result is that the mind will be created according to the lesser and more inferior conception of itself.

On the other hand, when all the actions of mind move toward the great within, the eye of the mind will concentrate upon the world of greater possibilities. The conception of things will in such a mental state constantly increase because attention at such times is concerned only with that which is larger and superior. Thus the mental energies will be directed towards the idea of superiority, and the creative energies will naturally rebuild the mind gradually and steadily upon a larger and more perfect scale. This is all very simple and anyone who will examine the workings of his own mind will find it to be absolutely true. We understand therefore how each individual has in his own hands the power to create for himself a greater mind, a more perfect personality, a richer life and a more desirable destiny.

In all methods for mental development this law must be wisely considered for no matter how perfect the method may be, if the mental actions move towards the surface, no results will be gained. While on the other hand, if the mental actions move towards the within results will positively be gained even though the methods be inferior. Nearly all minds in the past that continued to develop through life did so without system, but gained increase through aspiration, or rather concentration upon the greater possibilities of life, which in turn caused mental actions to move towards the within.

When your attention is turned upon the inner and the larger phases of life your mind will begin to turn its actions upon the great within. Accordingly all mental tendencies will begin to move toward superiority, and all the building forces in your life will have superiority as their goal. That you should constantly rise in the scale when thinking and acting in this manner is therefore evident. Remarkable results have been gained and can be gained simply through aspiration, but if a complete system of the best methods are employed in conjunction with the fundamental law, these results will naturally increase to a very great degree. For this reason all things that are conducive to the growth of the mind should be employed in harmony so that the increase of mental power may be gained in the largest possible measure.

To train the mental actions to move towards the within we should concentrate attention upon the greater possibilities of life, and think as deeply and as much as we can upon those possibilities. In fact we should train the mind to look towards the within at all times and view with great expectations those superior states that ere long will be attained. In addition all tendencies of life should be trained to move towards the higher and the larger and every thought should have an ascending spirit.

When you feel that you are becoming too much concerned with the superficial, turn attention at once upon the depths of existence. And when you feel that you have fallen down temporarily into the world of inferiority use every effort at your command to rise again towards the heights. The leading purpose should be to train all the forces, desires, tendencies and actions in life to move upward and onward at all times. This will cause the greater powers and possibilities within to be awakened, which will be followed by the perpetual increase of the capacity, the power and the quality of the mind. And with this increase conies also the increase of everything else in life that is required for our highest welfare.

When this increase of power begins it will naturally be felt in various parts of mind, and in order to know how to make the best possible use of this increase, as well as of the power we already possess, we should remember the great law, that whatever you feel that you can do, that you have the power to do. There are many methods through which we can determine what the mind really can do and what work we may be able to carry out successfully, but this particular law is the best guide of all, provided it is properly understood. And it is extremely important to discover what we are able to do because the majority are not in their true spheres of action.

To be in your true sphere of action means better work, greater results and more abundant good both to yourself and to others with whom you are associated. It also means that you can be at your best at all times and he who is at his best at all times is on the way to perpetual growth and perpetual increase.

To do your best work and your true work you must employ the largest and the strongest faculty that you possess. But to learn what this faculty actually is, this is the problem. This problem can be solved, however, if we live in compliance with the law just mentioned. The power that we possess is always felt, therefore when you feel that you can do a certain thing it means that there is sufficient power in that particular faculty that is required. But a faculty must be large before it can contain enough power to be consciously felt. Consequently the fact that you feel power in a certain faculty proves conclusively that faculty is large, and is possessed of considerable ability.

From this point on, the question to decide is, where you feel the greatest amount of power because where you feel the most power there you will find the greatest ability. This is conclusive, but here another question arises, that is, if the feeling of the average person is always reliable. The answer is that it is not. But it can be made so with a little training.

All psychologists have come to the conclusion that there is but one sense, the sense of feeling and that all other senses, both in the external and the internal are but modifications of this one sense. It is also admitted that the sense of feeling can be cultivated along scores of lines where it is now wholly inactive, and that there is no perceptible limit to its development along any line. This being true we shall go to the very foundation of all the senses, and all the modes of discerning things, when we take the sense of feeling for our guide in the selection of that work for which we have the greatest talent and power.

To train the sense of feeling in detecting the exact place in mind where the greatest power resides, the first step is to make this sense normal, which is highly important because the average person has so many artificial desires, and permits the mind to be stimulated by every successful venture that is heard of.

There are a great many people who become aroused with ambition to enter the literary world whenever they learn of remarkable success attained in that world. Thus their energies are temporarily turned upon the literary faculties and they feel considerable power in that part of the mind. This they think is sufficient evidence that they have literary talent and make attempts to get results in such work ; but they soon find that the inspiration in that direction did not last and they are compelled to try something else.

Then these people may learn of remarkable success in the business world. They become enthused over the possibilities of commercial ventures and turn their energies in that direction. But they soon find that their commercial faculties are not large enough to carry out their ambitions along this line. In consequence they turn their attention to the next venture that looks promising. There are thousands of minds who are constantly affected in this way, drifting from one thing to another. They imagine that because someone is succeeding in a certain work they may also succeed in that work, provided they have inclinations along that line. They also imagine that they are the very ones to enter every particular field where the demand for great service and great ability is required. The reason is their minds are controlled by appearances and what they feel as the result of the switching of energy here and there from one faculty to another. Such people therefore cannot rely upon the sense of feeling in any line of action because it is seldom normal.

To produce a normal sense of feeling for the purpose in question we should never pay any attention to what others have done or are doing because the success of others proves nothing as far as we are concerned. We must not look at the power of another man's brain, but try to find what there is in our own brains. We should never permit the enthusiasm of others to intoxicate our own minds. ,We should let others be enthused in their way and we should let them concentrate upon what work they like. But we should not imitate others either in thought, enthusiasm or feeling.

The course to pursue is to watch yourself closely for some weeks or months and try to discover in what faculty you feel the most power. If you feel the greatest power in a certain faculty and in that one only, you may choose that faculty without further examination and give it all your force, energy, ambition and desire, realizing that the application of that faculty will bring the greatest results that you could attain in your life. But if there are several other faculties that seem to be equally strong, wait and watch more closely until you finally discover the seat of the greatest power. When two or more seem to be equally strong, and continue thus under the most rigid self-examination, choose the one that you can use to the best advantage now, and turn all your power for attainment and achievement in that direction.

When there is prolonged uncertainty as to where the greatest amount of power is expressed try to increase the power of every part of your mind by directing the subconscious to express more power from within. The value of this is found in the fact that the greatest amount of power always goes to the largest faculty so that an increase of power will in every case reveal the existence of the leading talent or faculty in your possession.

After you have made the sense of feeling normal so that you can feel the state of your mind as it really is, you can always depend upon the law that whatever you feel that you can do you have the power to do. And you may proceed to act along that line knowing that you will succeed, no matter how difficult the undertaking may seem to be. It is the presence of great power in a certain faculty that makes you feel that you can do things by using that faculty. Therefore when you can feel what faculty is the largest and strongest you know positively what you can do, what you can accomplish and what you should undertake. True, a great deal of training of that strongest faculty may be required, but since the talent, the ability, and the power are there the results must follow when the practical application is made.

CHAPTER VIII.

THE WITHIN AND THE WITHOUT.

It has been stated that the average person is nine tenths environment; that is, nine-tenths of his thoughts, ideas, desires and motives are suggested by environment, or created in the likeness of what he has come in contact with in the outer life; and this is largely true. He is therefore almost wholly patterned after the things that make up his surroundings, and instead of being himself is a reflection of his circumstances. That such a person can master himself and control his destiny is out of the question because we cannot control external things so long as we are almost entirely in the control of those things.

When we analyze this phase of human life we find that the multitudes float with the stream like dead logs; therefore can never go where they wish nor accomplish what they wish. However, no life is complete until we can have things the way we like; that is, until we can consciously change ourselves and our environments according to those higher views of life that we are constantly receiving as we promote our progress. For this reason we must find some way that will lead us out from the control of environment if we wish to live a complete life and a life really worth living.

To proceed we find the law to be that anything in the without that is permitted to impress its likeness upon the mind will influence character, conduct, thought, action and living. And when you give such impressions full right of way they will actually control your life, the reason for which has been explained in preceding chapters. To avoid this influence from environment therefore, we must refuse to receive impressions from without that we do not desire. But since the greater part of these impressions come unconsciously the question will be how to avoid them. This question, however, is answered through the understanding of the law of receptivity.

It is natural for the mind to receive impressions from the without. It is also necessary. That is what the senses are for. But it is not natural to absorb through the senses all sorts of impressions from everything with which we may come in contact. When such impressions are absorbed without discrimination and without our cognizance of the fact we have a mental state called unconscious receptivity, and this state is produced by a weak character.

But here we must remember that a weak character is not necessarily a bad character ; because when you are very weak you may not even be able to do mischief. To be really bad you must be strong because a bad character is a strong mind misdirected, while a weak character is a negative sort of good ness, a goodness that means well but is wholly in competent. What is called character is that quality of mind that discriminates, selects, chooses and holds in possession what has been selected. Character therefore has two functions. The one selects the right and the other holds the mind in the right.

When character is absent or so completely negative that it is almost wholly inactive it is not possible for the mind to select the right or to hold the right. Such a mind will absorb nearly everything that environment may suggest and will therefore be a reflection of the present sphere of existence. Most minds have some character and therefore have a few ideas and motives of their own ; they accordingly eliminate some of the undesirable impressions that may try to gain entrance to the mind. But we are all aware of the fact that the average person is entirely too much under the influence of those things that surround him. The majority are affected to a large extent by surroundings, climatic conditions and atmospheres in general, though it is a sign of weakness to be influenced in this manner. The coming and going of events and the opinions of others also play a very large part in moulding the thought of most minds. But no mind should be modified by such influences unless he accepts those modifications by personal choice.

Every mind should be able to be himself, no matter what happens or fails to happen, and every mind should be able to think his own thought regardless of anyone's opinion on the subject. This, however, requires a strong character; that is, the ability to make your own selections and the power to stand by that which you have selected.

The attitude of receptivity has frequently been looked upon as a weakness, but it is the lack of character in this connection that constitutes the weakness. Receptivity in itself is indispensable. There are any number of illustrations to prove this fact. The mind that is not receptive to the finer things of life, such as music, art, love, the beauties of nature and so on, has not begun to live. Without the attitude of receptivity, however, no one can respond to anything.

But here we must remember that in becoming receptive we should train ourselves to respond only to such things as we consciously select. The most receptive mind has the greatest opportunities for enjoyment as well as for the increase of wisdom. But this receptivity must be guided, and character alone can do this. Receptivity must be employed consciously only, and unconscious receptivity must be entirely avoided.

The mind must be able to use consciously that to which it wishes to respond, and must also be able to respond perfectly when the choice is made. When such an attainment is secured you will always be yourself, you will never be influenced by anything but your own thought and you will get many times as much enjoyment out of those things of life that you are able to appreciate. And the path to such an attainment is a strong, highly developed character.

Continuing this study of man, and man's relations to his surroundings, we meet a metaphysical law of extreme importance, and it may be stated as follows : Man's welfare depends upon what he does in the within and how he relates himself to the without. The inner realm is the cause realm; therefore this inner realm must be acted upon consciously and properly when certain special effects are desired. But when these effects do appear the personal qualities through which they appear must be related correctly to their sphere of action.

There are many good effects that are spoiled because of discord in those personalities through which they appear, and there are many most excellent and most harmonious states of mind that remain unproductive because they are not supplied with the effect required. This proves that the within should act to the fullest degree possible and that the effects of all such actions should be placed in perfect harmony with external circumstances.

To promote the welfare of man all thought should be constructive and all outer relations should be harmonious. We should aim to agree with all adversaries. We should refuse to be out of harmony with anything or anybody. We should meet all things in their own world and meet them with the attitude of harmony towards their better side. And this we can do because it is possible to be harmoniously related to everything in life ; and what is more it is absolutely necessary. When true harmony is absent full expression is prevented, and since it is the bringing forth of the best alone that can give us the best, we find that the full expression of what is in us becomes indispensable to our highest welfare.

What we do in the within makes us what we are. And how we are related to the without determines what we are to receive from the world. When we do much in the within we become much, and the more we can accomplish and attain, or create, in our sphere of action. When we are properly related to the world we receive the very best from the world, that is, the best that we can appropriate, appreciate and use now. We can all understand therefore why man's welfare depends upon what he does in the within and how he relates himself to the without. However, to promote constructive action in the within we must learn to apply the law of growth in every part of the human mind, and we find that all growth and development is preceded by the expansion of consciousness. To expand consciousness therefore becomes one of the great essentials in everything that may pertain to perfect advancement and higher welfare.

Mental growth involves three stages unfoldment, development and cultivation; and in each stage new fields of action are appropriated. Whenever anything in the life of an individual is enlarged a new field of activity has been entered. Unfoldment is the bringing out into a larger sphere that which previously occupied a smaller sphere. Development is the multiplying of modes of action. And cultivation is the perfecting of those channels or vehicles through which the various modes of action may find expression. The term development is usually employed to cover the entire process because it merges with unfoldment on the subjective side and with cultivation on the objective side. Therefore when used by itself the entire process of growth is implied.

Since development in any sphere cannot take place until consciousness has been expanded in that sphere no process or system of development is complete until provided with practical methods for promoting stich expansion. This being true we see how inadequate modern systems of training must be; and accordingly it is not difficult to find numerous reasons why the race is not more highly developed.

However, any process of development will expand consciousness in a measure, provided the desire for expansion is held in mind when such a process is employed. But this desire must be present and must be very strong.

To try to feel the life of all life, or rather to place mind in conscious contact with all existence, will also promote the same purpose to a degree because in this attitude the mind actually transcends present limitations. In fact all limitations are eliminated in this way and the mind is set free to enter new regions whenever it may desire. This method, however, must be employed with wisdom and perfect self-control. There are many minds who have recently set themselves free from all limitations of consciousness through the exercise of universal sympathy; but not all have gained anything thereby. A few have been afraid to venture beyond what they already felt to be substantial, while others have roamed here and there and everywhere on the borderland of the unknown, wasting their energies in search of pastures green. They have had no definite aim except to find the new, and therefore have accomplished nothing. For the fact is that to find the new is not all that is necessary. When we find the new we must stop there awhile and get out of it what it may contain.

As a rule the imagination runs wild after limitations of consciousness have been removed, and only fragmentary impressions are gained whenever a slight pause for observation may be taken when in the midst of these new fields. The result is, ideas arid conclusions that have no foundation whatever, or opinions that seemed plausible to the one that produced them, but wholly devoid of truth, in fact mere freaks of aimless creative power. And it is a well known fact that such creations are entirely too numerous in the mental world at the present time. Imagination is a splendid servant, but as a master it will invariably lead you into chaos. And in the expansion of consciousness imagination is liable to take the lead unless controlled, because at such times it becomes intensely active.

To control the imagination at such times we should not permit it to do anything but construct the more perfect mental images according to such principles of life as have proven themselves to be scientifically true. The imagination should never be permitted to roam aimlessly. Whenever employed it should be put to work on something definite that you are resolved to perfect or work out.

Do not accept every new mental image as an exact truth, for a truth is usually represented by a large group of mental images. But such images cannot properly group themselves until the mind gets down to sound, rational md analytical thinking. It can therefore be stated as a fact that no mind really understands new ideas until its thinking concerning those ideas has been reduced to system.

In order to expand consciousness in any sphere, after the limitations of that sphere have been eliminated, the imagination must be controlled and the feeling of real life intensified. A highly active imagination, however, must be avoided because new ideas created by an act of the imagination does not necessarily indicate the expansion of consciousness because an active imagination is not always deep. It usually skims the surface or acts on the borderland of new fields and generally acts in the most haphazard manner. It is the quiet orderly imagination combined with deep feeling that indicates expansion of consciousness, and that actually creates new ideas that are really true as well as of actual worth.

When we proceed to expand consciousness we find that consciousness will not enter the new field until the faculty of interior insight has established the reality of that field. In other words, we must discern that the larger mental world is real before consciousness will proceed to work itself out into that larger world. For this reason we realize that all great minds must of necessity have interior insight, or that something within them that reveals the fact that the larger field is also sold ground.

The man who attempts great undertakings usually does so because he feels within him that success will crown his efforts. Something has told him that he can move out upon the beyond of present thought and action without any fear whatever. To the senses the new realms may look empty, and to venture on may appear to be nothing more than a wild leap into the fathomless abyss of utter destruction; but interior insight takes a different view.. This superior sight can see further and knows that the seeming void of the larger conscious field is actually solid rock. It also knows that this seeming void is rich with possibilities, many of which can be worked out in practical life now.

Interior insight may be defined as faith taking shape and form for practical action. Faith itself is a mental state that dwells constantly on the borderland of the unknown, while interior insight is a mental faculty the function of which is to examine things at a long range. Far sightedness among practical men of affairs is the same thing, and is one of the chief secrets of success in all important undertakings. Interior insight may be called the telescope of the human mind, and the more perfectly it is developed the better you understand the greater possibilities as well as the difficulties that lie before you.

It is therefore evident that when you have this insight you will know not only how to proceed, but also how to deal with those things that you know you will meet in your advancement toward greater achievements. When equipped with a well developed faculty of this kind you will know what to do to make all personal actions work together for the speedy realization of the greater things in store. In other words, you can plan ahead to advantage and you can turn all effort, thought and attention in the right direction. Many a time we fail to see the great opportunities that are almost within reach and instead of working up to them as we should if we saw them, we turn our efforts into channels that have practically nothing for us. Millions of mistakes of this kind have been made, but all of them could have been avoided through the use of interior insight.

According to the fact under consideration this insight must establish the reality of a new field before consciousness will naturally expand in that direction ; that is, it must prove to the mind that the new field is substantial and full of possibilities. The development of interior insight is therefore absolutely necessary to the promotion of all other kinds of development and without it neither great attainments nor great achievements are possible. But with it there is no mental field, however large or marvelous, that the mind may not finally enter, explore, acquire and possess.

CHAPTER IX.

FINDING YOUR PLACE IN LIFE.

According to the natural workings of things, man gravitates towards those environments that are the exact counterparts of his own active nature. This is invariably the law. However, those who are living in undesirable environments may not take pleasure in accepting the idea presented in this law. It is more agreeable to place the blame elsewhere. But the fact that your surroundings are ordinary does not necessarily prove that you are an inferior person, although it does prove that you have not brought forth into full action the superior qualities that you may possess.

Here we should remember that it is the active nature that determines the surroundings in which we are to be placed, and the active nature in most persons is a mixture of conflicting forces, many of which are constantly neutralizing each other, or disturbing each other, thus preventing the more desirable of those forces to produce such results as they have the power to produce.

In addition, we must remember the fact that a disturbed nature always attracts inferiority or is drawn into disagreeable conditions. When the active forces in your nature conflict and neutralize each other your nature becomes like a leaf in the whirlwind, and you may become a victim of all the unpleasant conditions you meet.

There are a number of people with high and strong powers who never meet anything but the dark side of things and the reason is that their active forces are in conflict. One desire goes this way and another that way. Some intentions are constructive while others move at random. Their objects in life are constantly being changed and what they build up one day is taken down the next. Thus we understand why such people fail to build for themselves such environments or surroundings as they have the power to build, and also why they are found in situations that are inferior to the best that may exist in their own nature.

If the average mind should look closely at his own nature and ask himself if all the forces of his being are moving constructively and harmoniously towards his one great goal, he would find that they are not. He would discover far more conflict in his own mind and consciousness than he expected, and he would have to admit that his surroundings are the exact counterpart of those things that are active in his own self.

There is one exception, however, to this rule, an exception that must be considered before we proceed further, and this exception is found in misdirected sympathy. We frequently find excellent people in environments where we know they do not belong. At first we may fail to discover the reason, and in failing to do this we may conclude that there is nothing in the idea that people attract their own environments, or are drawn into environments similar to themselves. But a close examination of these cases will reverse this conclusion. There are many people who remain where they are, and frequently in most undesirable environments, not because they belong there, but because their sympathy keeps them there. They do not wish to break away for fear others may suffer. We all know of many such cases, and when we look into this subject closely we find that misdirected sympathy is one of the greatest obstacles to the proper adjustment of persons with their true surroundings.

If it were not for misdirected sympathy several million people would today be living in far better environments environments that would be directly suited to their present natures and needs. But to break loose from old associations and accept new opportunities may at times seem unkind. However, we must remember that we are living for the whole race, and not only for a few friends. And also that we can render the best service to the race, including our present friends, by being perfectly true to ourselves ; that is, by living and working where we actually belong.

Sentimentalism and abnormal feelings have kept down thousands of fine minds, and compelled many a human flower to wither among weeds ; but this is always wrong. The entire race is kept back in a measure whenever a single worthy person is held down. Therefore we must seek to avoid such a circumstance whenever we can. Each individual must be permitted to be true to himself; and it is wrong for us to shed tears when a friend finds it necessary to go elsewhere to promote his progress.

You may be living today in uncongenial or unpleasant environments, or your work may call you where you know you do not belong; and there are several causes. You may be held where you are on account of misdirected sympathy. If so, give reason a chance to prove to you that you are wronging everybody by staying where you are. You can not do the right thing for yourself nor for anyone else unless you are at your best, and to do your best you must be where you belong.

Then you may be held where you are because you have no definite purpose in life, and if so, decide upon a purpose, proceeding at once to train all the forces of your being to work for that purpose and that alone. Gradually you will work away from your present surroundings and doors will open through which you may pass to better things. There is nothing that will take you into better environments more quickly than to have a fixed and high purpose, and to marshall all the powers of mind and soul to work together for the promotion of that purpose. And since this is something that all can do, there is no reason whatever why a single person should live in surroundings that are inferior to himself.

Then there is another reason, possibly the most important of all. You may be held where you are because your good qualities are negative and have neither working capacity nor practical application. If the better side of you is negative and if such adverse tendencies as you may have inherited are positive and active, you are making for yourself a world that is anything but ideal. In this case it is not the best that is in you, but the worst that is in you that determines what kind of surroundings you are to receive, build up or attract. However, when your better side becomes strong and positive ; when your good intentions are filled with living power, and when you turn all the forces of your being into the promotion of larger and higher aims, there is going to be a great change. You will soon begin to build for the better, you will begin to gravitate towards better environments and you will meet everywhere more congenial conditions.

But in this connection one of the great essentials is that all the forces of your better nature be in harmony and trained to work together for those better environments that you have in view. It is not what you are negatively, inherently or potentially that determines your present conditions in life. It is what you use and how that something is used. There are people with small minds and insignificant abilities that are now living in most desirable environments simply because the active forces of their nature work together for a definite object constantly in view. Then there are others with splendid minds and remarkable talents that are living in the midst of failure and distress simply because they did not make constructive use of the powers they possessed ; in other words, the better elements in their nature were not in harmony and therefore could not produce results.

It is strict adherence to the quiet, steady, orderly and constant forward movement that will bring you to the goal in view, and even when your forces are so weak that you have to move slowly. But when you are endowed with extraordinary capabilities you will through this process rise rapidly, and finally attain everything you have had in view. A man may not be strictly honest or moral, nevertheless, if he has ability and employs his faculties constructively and harmoniously, he will build for himself a superior environment. And through his power to achieve the greater things he will be attracted towards opportunities that will promote still further the improvement of his environment. But it must be remembered that if this man were honest, moral and true his power would be still greater, and he would enjoy far better the richness and beauties of his delightful surroundings.

There is a belief among many that honest people ought to have the best that life can give, but the mere state of being honest is not sufficient. The best man in the world will be a failure if he does not employ his ability constructively, because it is doing things that counts. And to do things the powers we possess must work in harmony and work with a definite object in view.

In this connection we must not forget that the mind that is pure, honest and just can accomplish far more with a given ability than one who does not have these virtues. Virtues do not create but they do have the power to give proper direction to the process of creation. It is constructive ability that does things. Character simply guides the doing so that the product may be of the highest order and the greatest worth. That the person, therefore, who has character only and no constructive ability will accomplish very little in the world and will have to submit to the inconsistencies of fate.

The course to pursue is to combine ability with character, and to turn all powers and talents towards the attainment of some definite goal. When we take this course we are going to rise out of our present conditions and enter steadily and surely into the better and the superior. It is your active nature that counts. You may have a score of good qualities, but if those qualities are not active they will contribute nothing to the building up of your environment or your destiny. Therefore the more development, the more power and superiority that you can express through your active nature, the greater will be the results in the external world.

But all the qualities of your active nature must have worth and must work together. Superior qualities working at variance with each other will take you down into inferior environments, while inferior qualities if constructive and united in action will take you into better environments than you may be living in now. The whole problem therefore is to express your best in action, and to train the active powers and qualities in your being to work in perfect harmony ; that is, to work together for the same purpose and in the same attitude.

Conflicting tendencies of mind have given poverty, distress and misfortune to many of great ability and superior goodness, while properly united tendencies have given success to many a man who was neither able nor true. However, nature is just. We receive according to what we have accomplished ; not according to what we have tried to do, but what we actually have done ; or in other words, not according to what there is in us, but according to how much of what is in us we applied in a thorough and practical manner.

We will receive material success and delightful exterior surroundings if we have worked properly for those things. But if we have neglected to work for the finer things of life we will receive nothing that has permanent value in human existence, and we will not have the capacity to enjoy our ideal surroundings. For this reason the wise man works for all that is beautiful and true, both in the material sense and in a higher sense. Accordingly he will receive riches both in the without and in the within ;thereby gaining the privilege to live the full life, the complete life and the life that is really worth living. You may conclude therefore that if things are not right in your world you are to blame. Accept the blame and resolve to take things into your own hands and make them right. This you can positively do because your environment will be exactly what your active nature is, and you can change your active nature as you may desire.

CHAPTER X.

WHEN ALL THINGS WORK FOR GOOD.

In analyzing the workings of the mind there is no subject of more importance than that of the relation of good and evil. Concerning evil there are many doctrines, some of which declare that it is a real and permanent power battling with the good, while others declare that it is nothing, or simply the absence of good. Then between these two extreme beliefs almost any number of other beliefs may be found. To prove that evil is an actual principle personified in some form is not only difficult, but impossible. On the other hand, to prove to the world that evil is nothing is by no means simplicity itself. Nevertheless, this doctrine comes very nearly being the truth.

However, it is not our purpose to analyze the nature of evil in this connection. That is a subject so large that separate attention would be required. Our object here is to make clear what we wish to bring out in connection with a most important law, viz., that when we give conscious recognition to the existence of an evil we tend to increase its power and multiply its effects. And in dealing with this law it will be necessary to define briefly what evil actually is, or rather what the new psychology has found it to be.

To say that evil is the absence of the good is not sufficiently explicit; while to say that evil is undeveloped good is simply to play upon words. The process of development is continuous ; therefore the fully developed of today is undeveloped in comparison with the possibilities of tomorrow. So that according to that idea the good of today would be evil in the light of tomorrow which is by no means a scientific idea. The truth in this connection is that when we employ the undeveloped just as if it were developed we produce what we call evil, and it is this fact that has given rise to the belief that evil is undeveloped good.

When we look closely at those things that are called evil we find that in every case force has been employed contrary to the natural laws involved. It will therefore be correct to say that evil is misdirected good, or that it is the improper use of a power that is in itself good. In fact, all powers, forces and elements are good in themselves because all that is real is good. Everything is created for a good purpose and is actually good, but it is possible to employ it for a purpose that is not in accord with those laws under which we live at the present moment. And here is where evil may arise.

Every act is good, proper and useful when performed in its own sphere of action, but when performed outside of its own sphere it is not good. It produces conditions that we call evil. This being true the fact that every act has its own sphere of action is one of the greatest facts in the universe. We can do only such things at such times that harmonize with the laws that obtain at the time and under the circumstance. And it is absolutely necessary to the persistence of the universe that such laws be absolute, because if they were not the universe would be chaos.

To simplify the subject we may state that evil is a condition produced by an act that is performed outside of its natural sphere, and that the power and effects of that condition depend upon how much life the mind throws into that particular act. It is a well-known fact that the mind gives its life to those actions and conditions upon which consciousness is directed, and consciousness is always directed where reality is supposed to exist. Therefore when we give conscious recognition to the existence of an evil we give more life and power to those conditions that we call evil, and in consequence make them much worse than they were. This is very simple because the more attention you give to anything the more life and power you add to that particular thing, be it good or evil. Accordingly it is unwise to give attention or recognition to evil under any circumstance.

However, the question is how we can prevent giving conscious attention to the evil and the wrong. When evil seems so very real how can we avoid giving conscious recognition to its existence ? The answer is that we must get a better understanding of the real nature of evil and the real nature of good, because when this understanding is gained we can train the mind to act correctly in this connection. When we know that evil is not a thing, not a principle, not a reality, but simply a certain temporary and mistaken use of reality; and when we know that the use of that reality has its origin in our own minds, our attention will at once be transferred from the unpleasant condition surrounding the evil, and be directed instead upon our own inner mental domain. Thus consciousness will be withdrawn from the condition called evil and will become concerned with the change of mental action. Accordingly the power of the evil will at once be diminished.

Actual experience in life has demonstrated the fact a number of times that pain or even a severe disease will disappear instantaneously when consciousness is fully and completely taken into another sphere or thought or action. This proves that an evil condition can live only so long as we give it life, and we give it life only so long as we consciously admit or recognize its existence. When an evil condition is felt, attention should at once be directed upon the opposite good that exists in the inner world of perfection. This action of the mind will take consciousness away from the unpleasant condition and will cause all the faculties of the mind to work in realizing the absolutely good.

When we proceed to trace all perverted action to its inner mental source consciousness will follow, leaving evil behind, and coming to give its life to the change of the said source which proves itself simply to be a misunderstanding of things. Then if the desire of the heart is to change the source of that action, or in other words, to gain a correct understanding of things, the new and the ideal image of the good will appear in the mind, and according to laws previously presented a change for the better will follow at once.

To illustrate, we will take a depressed condition of mind or body and proceed to remove it by this method. First, we will picture clearly upon the mind the perfect image of harmony so that we can almost see harmony with the mind. Second, we will prove to ourselves through reason that this depressed condition is not a thing, but the temporary result of valuable power misdirected. And since this power is misdirected by our own mind, our own mind must contain the origin of that misdirection. Then we will turn attention upon our own inner mentality with a view of removing the source of perversion, establishing a state of harmony; and while thus directing attention upon the inner mentality we will hold the mind in such an attitude that it is moving directly upon the image of perfect harmony.

The result will be that consciousness will become so absorbed in creating the new state of harmony that it will withdraw completely from the outer evil condition. This outer condition will in consequence disappear as it is deprived of life, while the new state of harmony will be firmly established by receiving all the attention and all the life. In other words, when consciousness leaves the condition of evil, has nothing further to live on, and will disappear ; and as consciousness enters the condition of harmony and good in the within those conditions will receive all the life that consciousness has to give, and will accordingly grow and develop until they become sufficiently strong to take possession of the entire human system.

This is a simple process that works perfectly and that can be employed successfully in removing any undesirable condition from mind or body. However, before we begin we must picture clearly upon the mind the image of the perfect state that we seek to realize and develop, and proceed as above in the elimination of the wrong through the creation of the right. A perfect understanding of the law under consideration will aid remarkably in turning our attention as required because there is nothing that can change the mind so readily as the reasoning process involved in a clear understanding of the subject at hand.

To realize fully that life and power always go wherever consciousness goes, is extremely important and also that consciousness can be directed anywhere by becoming thoroughly interested wherever we wish it to go. In applying these methods people who feel deeply always have the best results because deep feeling tends to produce deep interest in those conditions into which we wish to direct attention.

Closely connected with this process we find a most important metaphysical law which may be stated as follows: All things work together for good to him who desires only the good. And as it is possible for anyone to desire the good and the good only we realize that it is possible for anyone to cause all things to work together for good in his life. This law proves that the way to better things is not nearly as difficult as we have supposed it to be, and also that the straight and narrow path is by no means a path that the few alone can enter.

The doctrine of the straight and narrow path has been misinterpreted as it does not refer to something that is so extremely difficult to pass through, nor is it a path that leads directly away from everything that is pleasant in life. Neither is it so narrow that we can pass through it only when we have given up everything else in life. The belief that everything in life must be left out if we wish to take this path is not only absurd, but is the very opposite to the real truth. The path that leads into life, the full life, the complete life, the beautiful life is straight because it is established upon law. When you take this path you begin to use all the laws of life properly and will therefore gain all the good things that life has the power to give.

Here we must remember that a law is not a cruel something, the function of which is simply to pun- ish. A law is a path that leads to greater and better things. Therefore to follow a law is to move directly towards the better and the greater. When we live according to a law we are constantly receiving the greater riches that lie in that path, and when we live according to all the laws of life we receive everything good that life can give. However, when we violate law we go outside of the path, where there is nothing to be gained and nothing to live for. In fact, we step out of everything that pertains to life and thus enter chaos, the result of which is pain, loss and retrogression. It is not the law that gives us punishment when we go astray. When we go astray we deprive ourselves of the good things of life by going away from that path where those good things are to be found. And when we are deprived of the good, the good is absent ; and the absence of the good means evil, the entering into of which means punishment.

The path that leads into life is narrow because it gives room only for your own individuality, and only for the true self. You cannot be a double self, one part good and the other not, when you enter this path. There is only room for the true self. Neither can you lean on some one else. There is not room for anyone upon which to lean, as the path is for yourself alone. On this path you must live your own life and give all others freedom to live their own life.

Life is given us to be lived, and to live life we must live to ourselves according to our own light and our own individual needs. The path to life is the path to better things ; in other words, it is the advancing path and is therefore not a dismal, disagreeable or difficult path. On the contrary, it is the very opposite and is found by seeking the good and the good only. So long as we have only the good in mind we will be on this path. We will live according to the laws of life and will receive only good things because the laws of life can give only good things. But when we begin to desire what is not good we are at once drawn out of the path. Thus we will be deprived of the essentials of life, and instead we will enter into emptiness, weakness, perversion, confusion and all kinds of disaster.

When all our desires are directed upon the attainment of the highest good our creative powers will proceed to create and rebuild everything within us and about us, thus causing all things to become better. Everything in life will improve. We will be in more perfect harmony with our surroundings and will attract more agreeable persons, circumstances and events. We will become creators of the good. Everything that we do will produce good and everything that we attempt will result in good. We will meet all persons and environments on the better side, and will in consequence receive the best things that such persons and environments have the power to give. Every change that we make will be an open door to greater good because we are moving towards the good and the good only as every change is being made.

Here it is very important to remember that when we desire only the good we are always moving towards greater good, and must without fail realize the greater good in the near future. If we pass through a few unpleasant experiences while we are waiting we must not pay attention to such seeming inconsistencies. The fact that all will be well when we reach the goal in view should so fully occupy our minds that we will not be disturbed by any defect that may be found in the way over which we must for the present pass.

To desire the good, however, does not mean to desire mere self-satisfaction. It is the universal good that must be held in mind, the greatest good for everybody. And this must not only be held in mind but deeply desired with the whole heart and soul. The proper course is to desire only the high- est good and then turn all the life and power we possess into that desire. In fact we should make that desire far stronger than all other desires and we should live in it constantly.

As you proceed in this manner all the laws of the mind will work with you in promoting the realization of the good that you have in view and will gradually eliminate the results of past mistakes. Should the personal self tend to make new mistakes or take missteps, thereby leading your plans out of the true path, something will occur to prevent you from doing this before it is too late. The laws of your being will cause something to come in your way and thus turn your life in another direction, that is, in a new direction where the highest good you have in view may be finally realized.

When you have set your heart and soul upon the attainment of the good and the good only, the predominating powers in your being will work only for good, and all lesser powers will, one after the other, be taken into the same positive current so that ere long all things in your life will work together for good. We may not understand at first how these powers operate, but we shall soon find that the results we had in view are being realized more and more. And as this realization is gained we shall come positively to the conclusion that all things do work together for good when we desire the good and the good alone.

CHAPTER XI

WITH WHAT MEASURE YE METE.

He who gives much receives much. This we all know, but the question is what it means to give. When we speak of giving we usually think of charity and poverty ; and believing that the latter is inevitable we conclude that the former must be an exalted virtue ; but poverty is not inevitable. It is not a part of life's plan. It is simply a mistake. Therefore charity cannot be otherwise than a temporal remedy. Such remedies, however, though good and necessary, do not always constitute virtues because virtue is permanent and is a part of a continuous advancement in man.

He who gives in charity does not receive anything in return unless he also gives himself. It is therefore not the giving of things that brings reward, but the giving of life. But to give much life one must possess much life, and to possess much life one must live a large measure of life. According to the law, life is measured out to us with the same measure that we employ in the measuring of our own existence. In other words, we will receive only as much life as our own measure can hold ; but it is not only life that is measured out to us in this way. Everything that pertains to life is measured in a similar way.

We conclude, therefore, that he who sets out a large measure to be filled will receive a large measure full, and that he who gives himself simply offers his own life for further enrichment. He who gives much of himself will be abundantly enriched because he places in life a large measure of himself to be filled. He who gives things may lose all that is given. But he who gives himself, the best that is in himself, loses nothing. Instead he gains a larger and a richer self. He who gives himself to the race gives life and life can supply all needs.

To have an abundance of life is to have the power to help yourself and to recreate your own world according to your highest desires. The gift of life is therefore the highest gift. It is also the largest gift because it includes all gifts. He who gives life does not give to relieve poverty, but to build strong souls, and when strong souls appear poverty disappears of itself. To give one's life is to express in thought, word or action everything of worth that one may possess in mind or soul ; that is, everything that one may live for. And how much we live for depends upon how largely the life is measured in our understanding. When we measure life largely, life will give us a large measure of itself.

When we blend consciousness with the universal we will receive universal consciousness in return. When we think only of the boundless, our thought will be limited no more. When we take a larger measure of our talents the wisdom that fills the universe will also fill that larger measure. When we take a large measure of man and have faith in the superior side of every mind, every mind will give to us as much as our measure of that mind can hold. Realizing these great facts we should dwell constantly in the world of greater possibilities.

We should expect much, work for much, live for much, have faith in much, and we shall find that as much will come to us as we have thought, lived and worked for. We should never limit anything nor anyone. The measure of all things should be as large as our conscious comprehension and we should refuse to be contented with anything except that which is constantly enlarging its measure. Accordingly we should live for great things and press on. Thus the greater and the greater will surely be measured out in return. This is the law and it cannot fail.

Very few, however, apply this law and that is the reason why the majority accomplish so little. They undertake so little and they never reach the high places because they nearly always aim at the low ones. Many minds that aim high for a while lose their lofty aspirations later on because they fail to reach the mountain top the first week or the first year. Others again aspire to the high things though at the same time think of themselves as limited, insignificant and even worse. But if we would become great we must blend all though with greatness and measure ourselves with that measure that is large enough to contain all the greatness we can possibly conceive of.

He who expands consciousness so as to measure things largely gains capacity, while he who takes a small view of everything remains incompetent. We do not get power, growth or ability by trying to cram a small mind, but by trying to expand the mind. And to expand the mind we must take the largest possible view of all things. We must live with the limitless and blend all thought with infinite thought. When the senses declare you cannot do this, reply by saying, It is in me to do it ; therefore I can.

While the person is working with the limitations of the present, the mind should transcend those limitations and constantly take larger measures of both life and attainment. And as soon as this larger measure is taken the larger will begin to appear until even the person is called upon to enter a larger work with increased remuneration. Make yourself worthy and greater worth will come to you. Take a larger measure of your own capacity, your own ability, your own worth. Expect more of yourself. Have more faith in yourself and that something that supplies everybody will completely nil your measure.

It is the law that no matter how large your measure will be it will be filled. And your measure of things is as large as your conscious realization of those things. Therefore to take a larger and a larger measure of anything is to expand consciousness beyond the present understanding of that particular thing. Therefore all that we are conscious of is but a partial expression of something that is in itself limitless because everything in existence is limitless. Therefore by gaining a larger consciousness of those partial expressions we will become conscious of a larger expression. And a larger expression of those things will appear through us, which means that our own life has been enlarged and enriched. This is all perfectly simple and proves conclusively why the boundless measures out to each individual only as much as the measure of that individual can hold.

But since there is nothing to hold consciousness in bounds except our own limited view, and since we can take a larger view of anything whenever we choose, it is in our power to increase the measure of anything in our own life or in our own sphere of existence. Perpetual increase and perpetual expansion of consciousness go hand in hand in the life of man. The former is produced by the latter and the latter is produced by man himself. We conclude, therefore, that anyone can make his life as large as he wishes it to be, and can bring into his life as much of everything as he may desire.

In considering this great subject we must give due attention to the process of growth. And in this connection we must remember that the desire for growth and the effort to promote growth must be constant. This law, however, is frequently neglected as it is the tendency of nearly every person to lean back, fold arms and suspend all desire and every effort whenever a victory has been won, or an onward step taken. But we can never afford to stop or to suspend action at any time and what is more it is impossible to suspend action.

We cannot stop living, therefore we cannot stop thinking, and so long as we think, some part of our being will act. And that part should act with some definite goal in view. When you leave the field of action to rest, so to speak, you permit that part of your being that does act to act aimlessly, and aimless actions always produce perversions, false states and detrimental conditions. It is the conviction of every thorough student of life that aimless action is the fundamental cause of all the ills that appear in life. And aimless action is caused by the attempt to stop all action when we try to rest. However, the fact that action will go on perpetually in some part of our system proves that the individual Ego should be constantly at hand to guide that action.

The Ego does not need any rest, nor need it ever suspend activity, because rest simply means recuperation, and it is those organs that receive and use up energy that require recuperation. The Ego does not create and does not employ energy, but simply governs the distribution and use of energy. So that the real you should always be active in some sense, and should always desire the promotion of growth as well as carry out the promotion of growth, regardless of how many special parts of your system have suspended action for the time being.

When we understand the real purpose of rest we perceive clearly why the governing conscious Ego requires no rest whatever, and also why it does require ceaseless conscious action. To prevent aimless action the Ego should guide action on the mental or spiritual plane whenever rest demands suspension of activity on the physical plane. It has been demonstrated conclusively that the body rests most perfectly when some constructive action takes place in mind or soul, and it is for this reason that the first day of the week has been consecrated to the spiritual life. By giving this day entirely to higher thought, and the contemplation of the finer things of life, the body and the mind will recuperate so perfectly that you can do more work and far better work during the coming week than ever before ; although not simply because you have properly rested mind and body, but also because you have through your higher devotions awakened new life, more life and a number of higher, stronger powers.

The principle that the body rests most perfectly when consciousness is actively at work on some higher plane is a principle that should receive the most thorough attention, and every person should adopt some system of living by which this principle could be carried out completely in every detail. Such a system of living would prolong the life of the body, increase the power of the mind and remarkably unfold the soul.

The metaphysical law under consideration is based upon this principle. Therefore to live according to this principle, this law must be constantly employed; that is, the desire for growth and effort to promote growth must be constant. In addition, the desire for growth must be constructive because no action is constructive unless it is prompted by the desire for growth. And every effort to promote growth must be constant, because efforts that do not aim at growth are destructive, while suspended efforts cause aimless action. To carry out this law transfer your desire for growth from one faculty to another, and from one plane to another, as conditions may demand, or as your work may require, but never suspend that desire.

When you feel that a certain faculty, through which you have been acting, needs recuperation withdraw action from that faculty and begin to act through another faculty, expressing through this other faculty all the desire for growth that you can possibly create. Or, when you feel that the physical plane needs recuperation act upon the mental. When both mental and physical planes require recuperation enter the spiritual and express there your desire for soul unfoldment. Then whenever you express your desire for growth do something to promote that growth use what methods you possess and gradually you will evolve better and more effective methods.

As you apply all these ideas, consciousness will constantly expand, development will be constantly taking place in some part of your being, and you will be improving in some way every minute. In addition, you will prevent all aimless action and all retarded growth. Every part of the system will receive proper rest and recuperation whenever required, and this will mean complete emancipation because all ills come from aimless action, retarded growth and their consequences. It will also mean greater achievements and higher attainments because all the faculties will improve steadily and surely, and the entire system will be at its best under every circumstance.

CHAPTER XII.

FINDING MATERIAL FOR MIND BUILDING.

To live is to move forward but there can be no forward movement without new experience. Therefore in all advancement, in all progress, in all attainment, in all achievement, and in the living of life itself experience is indispensable. Experience being necessary to the promotion of advancement as well as to the increase of the value and the welfare of life, it becomes necessarily a permanent and continuous cause in the world of every individual, and as like causes produce like effects, both in quality and in quantity, experience should be sought and selected with the greatest possible care.

It is also highly important that we seek an abundance of experience because so long as the cause has quality it cannot be too extensive in quantity. Experience is the material from which character and mentality are constructed. Therefore the richer and more abundant our experience, the stronger and more perfect will our character and mentality be- come. Everything has its purpose and the real purpose of experience is to awaken new forces, new states, new phases of consciousness, and to originate new actions in the various parts of being.

To unfold and bring forth what is latent in the being of man is the principal object of experience. And it is well to remember that without experience no latent quality or power can ever be aroused and expressed. The power of experience to bring forth what is latent and to originate the new gives cause to enjoyment and happiness, as well as progress, and since experience is the only cause of enjoyment, it follows that what the enjoyment is to be in the life of any individual will depend directly upon what experience that individual will select.

The average mind makes no effort to select experience wisely, therefore fails to promote the real purpose of experience; and failing in this he also fails to awaken and develop those things in himself that can produce the most desirable of all experience, that is, the consciousness of a perpetual increase of all that has real worth in life.

The more experience the better, provided it is rich, constructive and wholesome, though no person should seek experience for the mere sake of passing through experience. The belief that experience it- self builds life is not true, nor is there any truth in the doctrine that all kinds of experience, good and otherwise, are necessary to the full development of life. It is only a certain kind of experience that can add to the welfare of life and promote the purpose of life. Therefore to understand the psychology of experience and how experience is connected with the workings of mind is a matter of exceptional importance.

The daily purpose of each individual should be to seek the richest experience possible in order that the best material possible may be provided in the building of himself. To this end he should place himself in daily contact with the best that is moving in the world, and the more of this the better. Such a practice will develop the mind, perfect the character, refine and re polish the personality, and increase perpetually the health and the wholeness of the body. It will also tend directly towards the promotion of a long and happy life.

The mind should be wideawake to everything in its sphere of existence that can give expression to superior action; and seek to gain the richest possible experience by coming in contact with that action. To place one's self in mental contact with the best that is in action in the world is to originate similar actions within one's own mentality. These will arouse the superior forces that are latent in the deeper mentality and ere long a superior mental life will have been evolved.

The more experience that the mind can gain by coming in contact with the best things that are alive in the world the larger, the broader and the more perfect will the mind become. It is therefore evident that the recluse must necessarily have a small mind whether he lives in the world or apart from the world. To live a life of seclusion is to eliminate experience to the smallest degree possible and there by cause the mind to become so small that only a mere fraction of its power and intellect can be unconscious action. In consequence such a person can never be his best in anything, not even in a single isolated talent, nor can his ideas as a whole have any practical value, being based wholly upon one sided opinions. In this connection it is most important to understand that the philosophy of the hermit is useless in practical life. And the same is true of moral or physical views as formulated by those who live in seclusion. Such ideas may look well in theory and they may be accepted by millions of people, but nothing outside of mere intellectual satisfaction will be gained. Intellectual satisfaction, however, when not directly associated with physical, mental and moral progress is detrimental; the reason being that it produces a phase of mental contentment which culminates in mental inactivity.

The only intellectual satisfaction that is normal and that can be beneficial, is that satisfaction which comes from the consciousness of continuous advancement. Any other satisfaction means mental inaction, and mental inaction leads to death invariably, not only in the intellectual but also in body, mind and character.

Those who live in the world and who are daily required to meet the problems of the world should seek guidance and instruction when necessary only from those superior minds that have had experience in the world. Those who live apart from the world do not appreciate the conditions that exist in the world. They have not been awakened to the real nature of those conditions. Therefore the solution that they may offer for the problem which may arise from such conditions can be of no practical value. He alone really knows who has had experience, though experience is not the whole of knowledge. It is only a small part, but that part is indispensable.

Minds that live only for themselves or for a selected few only, will also become narrow in mentality and dwarfed in character. Such living invariably results in retrogression because too many of the elements of life, both physical and metaphysical, are compelled through the lack of experience to remain inactive. The entire mentality and the entire personality should be active, and to promote such activity the entire individual life should be entirely filled with rich, wholesome and intellectual experience.

In brief we should live while we live and not simply exist. The lives of young people in particular should be well provided with an abundance of wholesome amusements and of every imaginable variety, though this practice should not cease with the coming of the thirties. We should all enjoy this life to the fullest extent so long as we remain in this life, though not simply because it is the privilege of us all to enjoy every moment to the fullest extent, but also because there are few things that are more conducive to wholesome experience than that of wholesome enjoyment. We gradually grow into the likeness of that which we enjoy. An abundance of wholesome amusement therefore will invariably produce a wholesome nature. And by enjoying the greatest possible number of the best things we shall naturally and steadily develop the best that is latent within us.

Every experience that we pass through awakens something within us that was not active before, and this something will in turn impress upon the subconscious the nature of the thought that was created during the experience. In fact the nature of the experience will determine what is to be awakened in the conscious mind and what is to be impressed upon the subconscious. And since subconscious impressions determine the character, the mentality and the personal nature of man, it is of the highest importance that only such experiences be selected as are rich, constructive and wholesome.

What is awakened in the mind of man is awakened by experience alone. For this reason no change in the mind can take place, unless preceded by some experience whether that experience be tangible or imaginary. And what is awakened in the mind of man determines first what he is to think, and second what he is to do and to be. These facts prove conclusively that experience is the material from which character and mentality are constructed. And therefore experience should receive the most thorough consideration during every period of life, and especially during the first twenty-four years of personal existence.

The experience that a person passes through during this early period will determine to a very great extent what is to be accomplished in later years ; the reason being that the early tendencies are the strongest as a rule, be they good or otherwise. We are not inferring, however, that man cannot change his nature, his character, his mentality, his habits, his desires or his tendencies at any time, because he can. But time and energy can be put to better use in later life than to that of overcoming the results of mistakes that could have been avoided if the proper mental tendencies had been produced early in life.

We should take advantage of favorable periods when we have them, and we should create such periods when we do not have them. This we can do, but when they come of themselves, as they do in the early years of personal existence, everything possible should be done to make these periods become a permanent power in our favor.

To permit the young mind or any mind to pass through experiences that are unwholesome or adverse is to cause tendencies to be produced that will work against him all his life, that is, if those tendencies are not removed later on, and they usually are not. But to limit the supply of experience at this period or at any period is equally detrimental. That person who enters the twenties in the consciousness of an abundance of rich experience is prepared for his career, and if he has a fair degree of ability he will succeed from the very beginning. He is ripe, so to speak, for his work. His mind has found normal action in nearly all of its phases and he will make but few mistakes of any consequence. It is totally different, however, with that person who has entered the twenties in what may be called the green state. Even though his mind may be highly active he will accomplish but little, because being as yet unconscious of his real nature, his real capacity and his true state of normal action, he will misdirect most of his energies and they will be used up before his success can begin.

The mind that lacks experience does not know its own power, its own possibilities, its own desires nor its own natural sphere of action. It has not found its bearings, and even though it may have remarkable ability it will invariably misplace that ability, and will in consequence fail utterly where lesser minds, with an abundance of wholesome experience to begin with, have nearly everything their own way.

It is therefore evident that the practice still prevalent in thousands of homes of compelling young people to be ignorant of what is going on in the world is most detrimental to the future welfare of those people. Such a practice has caused many a young mind to be a complete failure until he was thirty-five or more, though if he had received an abundance of wholesome experience early in life he could easily have entered into real success more than ten years before. An abundance of rich experience secured early in life will awaken the best that is in the person. He will thus become acquainted with himself and will know what to do with himself. He will also know what to do with others and how to apply himself in the outer world. However, we must remember in this connection that it is not necessary for anyone to do wrong or to mix with the wrongs of the world in order to gain experience. The fact is that such experience is not experience simply a misuse of mind, thought and action. The proper kind of experience is just as necessary to the young mind as the proper kind of education, and parents should in no way eliminate the opportunities of their children to gain experience of value and worth. But they should not let their children loose, so to speak, without paying any attention to the kind of experience that children seek to enjoy. To pass through experience that is neither rich nor wholesome is to cause tendencies, desires, habits and traits to be formed that are adverse to everything worth while that the person may try to do. The results of such experience will have to be removed before real living and real achievement can begin.

All young minds should be given the freedom to enjoy every imaginable form of enjoyment that can be found, provided such enjoyments are wholesome. And here we should remember that those young people who stay at home ignorant of the world are not any better in character than those who go out to enjoy the best that is living and moving in the world. And as to mental power they are much weaker than those who have come in contact with the movements of life and thought in all its phases. Moral purity does not come from keeping the mind in a state of inaction, nor does goodness come from the absence of desire. The best way to make the mind pure and the character strong is to give the person so much rich and wholesome experience that he will not care for that which is inferior or perverted. No normal mind will care for the lesser after he has gained possession of the greater. And those minds that are not normal do not need ethics, they need a physician.

An abundance of wholesome and most interesting enjoyment may be found anywhere, and the supply will increase with the demand. It is possible for any person to go out and come in contact with the world without going wrong, and the experience is invaluable, not only in a practical way but also in a way that touches the very cause of everything that has worth in the being of man. The more constructive experience that a person passes through the larger will the mind become and the more substantial will everything become that is active in his nature. An abundance of rich experience will invariably be followed by a larger subconscious life and this will add remarkably to the power and capacity of every talent and faculty. Such experience will also tend to give every force in the system the proper direction and thus prevent the waste of energy. The more experience we seek the better, provided that experience is sought for the purpose of awakening the larger and the better that is latent within us. And since experience in some form is absolutely necessary to the promotion of this awakening, the art of securing experience becomes a fine art, in fact one of the finest and most important in the world.

Every experience produces a subjective impression and when a number of such impressions of the highest order are secured there is not only a feeling of completeness and satisfaction that is beyond price, but the entire individuality gains a marked degree of superiority and worth. An abundance of rich experience will also give a substantial foundation to the mind, a foundation that no circumstance, however trying, will be able to disturb. And so long as the foundation of the mind is secure the various elements and forces of the system will be able to perform their functions well, no matter what temporary conditions may be.

One of the greatest secrets of success in any undertaking, or in any vocation in life, is found in the possession of a mental foundation so strong and so substantial that it is never disturbed under any circumstance. And as the right kind of experience will tend to build such a mental foundation, we realize the extreme value of the subject under consideration.

To feel that you have received your share of the good things that have come your way is one of the rare joys of life. And this feeling comes invariably from the subjective memory of rich and abundant experience. This feeling produces the consciousness of mental wealth and without it life is not complete ; but with it any person can pass through physical poverty and not feel poor in the least. While the mind that has had little or no experience is poverty stricken, no matter how extensive external possessions may be. Such a mind is practically empty, it finds no satisfaction in life and is incapable of turning its energies into constructive action. In brief, it flows with the stream and is almost completely in the hands of fate.

Experience, however, in the true sense is not synonymous with hardship. And to pass through trials and tribulations does not necessarily mean to gain experience. Occasionally it does, but as a rule it does not, and real experience awakens new life. It gives new points of view and enlarges the mental world. Instead of crushing individuality as hardships sometimes do it strengthens individuality, and makes the man more powerful both in mind and character than ever before. ,

To enjoy real experience, therefore, is not simply to pass through certain mental or physical conditions, but it is to gain something of permanent value while passing through those conditions. Experience of this kind may sometimes be gained through mistakes ; that is, when the mistake causes the mind to seek the other way; otherwise the mistake does not produce experience of value, and nothing is gained. However, it is not necessary to make mistakes or to go wrong in order to gain valuable experience. Neither is hardship, pain nor adversity necessary to growth, progress and advancement.

The most valuable experience comes, not through mistakes, but through the mind's sympathetic contact with the best that is alive in the world. Such experiences, however, may not be had for nothing. But to employ a small percentage of one's earnings in procuring such experiences is to make a most excellent investment. The bank of rich and whole some experience pays a very large interest. It will be profitable, therefore, for everybody to deposit as much as can be spared every week in this great bank. To keep in constant touch with the best that is living and moving in the world will give new ideas, new mental life, greater ambition, greater mental power, increased ability and capacity, and will in consequence increase the earning capacity of the individual. It will also increase the joy of living and make every individual life more thoroughly worth while.

The good things in the world, however, should not be sought for mere pastime. They should invariably be sought for the purpose of gaining conscious possession of the richness which they may contain.

This will increase immeasurably the enjoyment of the experience, and will cause the experience to add directly to the power, the quality, the worth and the value of life. It will make living more and more worth while, and nothing is worth more.

CHAPTER XIII.

BUILDING THE SUPERIOR MIND.

According to the conclusions of experimental psychology the possibilities that are latent in the soul of man are both limitless and numberless. It is evident therefore that when we learn to draw on the abundance of the great within we can readily build within ourselves all the elements of a superior mind. In applying this idea, however, the first essential is to recognize the fact that every effort to build for greater things must act directly upon the soul, because the soul is the only source of that which is expressed or that which may be expressed in the human personality.

In trying to build the superior in mind, life and character two methods have been employed. The first has been based upon the belief that man is naturally imperfect in every part of his being and that advancement may be promoted only by improving upon his imperfect qualities. The other method, which is the new method, is based upon the principle that man contains within himself all the qualities of superiority in a perfect state and that advancement is promoted, not by trying to improve upon his imperfections, but by trying to bring forth into personal expression more and more of the many perfect qualities that already exist within him.

The first method is necessarily a failure. And the reason why the race has improved so slowly is because this method has been used almost exclusively. A few, however, have in all ages, consciously or unconsciously used the second method, and it is through the efforts of these, that the advancement that we have made has been brought about. That the first method must be a failure is clearly understood when we realize that nothing can be evolved unless it is involved, and that it is impossible for man to bring forth the more perfect unless the more perfect already exists in a potential state within him.

This principle is well illustrated by the fact that we cannot produce light by acting upon darkness, nor produce perfection by trying to improve upon such things as do not have the possibilities of perfection. We cannot develop quality, worth or superiority in ourselves unless those elements which go to make up qualities of worth and superiority already exist within us. Development means the bringing out of that which is already within. But if there is nothing in the within no development will take place, no matter how faithfully we may apply ourselves. Thus we realize that before development along any line can be promoted, we must recognize the fact that we already possess within us all those elements that may be needed for the promotion of that development even to the highest possible degree. In other words, we must recognize the fact that all the possibilities of perfection already exist within us, and that we are therefore in reality perfect through and through as far as our real or in- terror nature is concerned.

Those who employ the first method do not recognize the greater possibilities within and therefore they do not try to bring forth what is already within them. They simply try to improve the imperfect in their personal nature by acting upon the imperfect. But we cannot fill an empty space by simply acting upon emptiness. We must bring something into that empty state if we wish fullness to take place. The imperfect lacks something; that is the reason why it is imperfect. And that something must be supplied from some other source before improvement or change for the better can be brought about. That something, however, that is lacking may be found in the great within because the great within contains everything that man may require to produce perfection in any part of his mind, character or personality.

The possibilities of the within are limitless and numberless. Of this fact we have any amount of evidence. Therefore by adopting the second method for building the superior in the human mind it is evident that any individual may steadily rise in the scale until he finally reaches the high goal of attainment that he may have in view.

To proceed, realize that the source of perfection and the source of all the elements of quality and worth exist already within you. Then by becoming more deeply conscious of these superior qualities that you possess within yourself those qualities will be expressed more and more, because the law is, that whatever we become conscious of within ourselves that we shall naturally express through mind and personality.

If you wish to improve any faculty or talent realize that the interior foundation of that faculty is perfect as well as limitless, and that you can make that faculty as remarkable as you wish by unfolding the perfection and the limitless power that is back of, beneath, or within that faculty. There is nothing to be gained by trying to patch up, so to speak, the imperfections of the exterior side of mind or personality through the application of some superficial or artificial method, though this is practically all that modern systems of mind building have attempted to do.

When we examine the results of those systems we realize how futile such methods necessarily are in this connection. However, when we proceed to enlarge the actual capacity of a faculty by drawing upon the interior and limitless source of that faculty we secure something with which to work. And by employing a scientific system of objective training in addition to the perpetual enlargement of a faculty from within, we build up not only a powerful faculty, but we learn to apply all of its power and talent in practical use.

The same methods will hold in the building of any part of the mind or the whole of the mind. And it is such methods through which we may secure not only satisfactory results in the present, but a perpetual increase of results for an indefinite period. Before we can employ these methods, however, we must recognize the fact that the real man within is already perfect and limitless and that the subconscious root of every talent or faculty is also perfect and limitless.

Therefore our object must not be to perfect our external selves by trying to improve upon our external selves regardless of what we may possess within us, but our object must be to bring forth into expression an ever increasing abundance of the power, the quality and the worth that is already latent within us. We must live, think and act with this great purpose uppermost in mind regardless of circumstances. In fact, everything we do must be done with the desire to bring forth more of the wonderful that is within us. And it is in this way that we may build the superior mind.

Those who have gone beneath the surface of mere existence and have familiarized themselves with real life know that the personal man is as he thinks. Therefore to perfect the personal man thought must be more perfect. But here we must remember that thought is created in the likeness of our own conception of ourselves. Therefore, so long as we think that we are imperfect in every part of body, mind and soul it is natural that our thought will be imperfect, and the personal man will accordingly in body, mind and character continue to be imperfect.

The law is that thought is the cause of every state or condition that appears in mind, character or personality. Thus we realize that so long as we think of ourselves as imperfect we will create imperfect thoughts; and imperfect thought will produce nothing else but imperfect conditions and states in every part of our being.

However, when man discovers that he himself in the real and in the soul state of his existence is absolutely perfect, he will think of himself as perfect, that is, he will not consider himself as an imperfect personality, but constantly think of himself as an individuality possessed of all the elements, powers and qualities of the highest state of perfection. Accordingly his thought will be perfect as far as he has developed this higher conception of himself. And since the personal man is in his nature the result of thought, more and more perfection will accordingly be expressed in every part of the personal man.

As man grows in the understanding of his own interior perfection his thought of himself will be higher and higher, better and better, more and more perfect. His mind, body and character will in consequence improve in proportion. And since there is no limit to the latent possibilities of perfection any individual can by attaining a larger and deeper conscious realization of the perfect qualities within develop himself perpetually, because whatever we become conscious of within ourselves that we naturally express through the life of the personality.

The art of building the superior in the human mind as well as in personality and character is therefore based upon the discovery that the real interior man is not only perfect in all his latent elements and qualities, but is actually a marvelous being; in fact is within himself limitless in power, having superior qualities that are actually numberless.

To unfold these possibilities and gradually bring out into expression more and more of the marvelous man within, we must become more and more conscious of this power and worth and perfection that exists within us. And this consciousness may be attained by thinking constantly with deep feeling of this interior perfection ; and also by actually living for the one purpose of unfolding more and more of this interior perfection.

In brief, the principle is this: The superior already exists within us. When we become conscious of the superior we will, according to a leading metaphysical law, express the superior; and what we express in mind or personality becomes a permanent part of the personal man. Mind building, therefore, is based upon the bringing out of the greatness that is within, and in learning to apply in practical life that power which naturally comes forth, through mind and personality, as this interior greatness is unfolded.

CHAPTER XIV.

THE SECRET OF THE MASTER MIND.

The mind that masters himself creates his own ideas, thoughts and desires through the original use of his own imaging faculty, while the mind that does not master himself forms his thoughts and desires after the likeness of impressions received through the senses; and is therefore controlled by the conditions from which those impressions come, because as we think so we act and live. Accordingly the master mind is a mind that thinks what he wants to think regardless of what circumstances, environments or associations may suggest.

The average mind desires what the world desires without any definite thought as to its own highest welfare or greatest need, the reason being that a strong tendency to do likewise or to imitate is always produced in the mind when desires are formed in the likeness of impressions that are suggested by external conditions. It is therefore evident that a person who permits himself to be affected by suggestion will invariably form artificial desires. And to follow such desires is to be misled in every instance. The master mind, however, desires only that which is conducive to real life here and now and in the selection of those desires is never influenced in the least by the desires of the world.

The power of desire is one of the greatest of all powers in the human system. It is therefore highly important that every desire be normal and created for the welfare of the individual himself. But no desire is normal that is formed through the direct influence of suggestions. Such desires are always abnormal and cause the individual to be misplaced.

This explains why a very large number of people are misplaced. They do not occupy those places wherein they may be their best and accomplish the most. They are working at a disadvantage and are living a life that is far inferior to what they are intended to live, and because of abnormal desires. They have imitated the desires of others without consulting their own present need. They have formed the desire to do what others are doing, permitting their minds to be influenced by suggestions and impressions from the world, forgetting what their present state makes them capable of doing now. Thus, by living the lives, the habits, the actions and the desires of others they are led into a life not their own; in other words, they are misplaced.

The master mind is never misplaced because he does not live to do what others are doing, but what he himself wants to do now, and he wants to do only that which is conducive to real life, a life worth while, a life that steadily works up to the very highest goal in view.

The average mind requires a change of environment before he can change his thought. He has to go somewhere or bring into his presence something that will suggest a new line of thinking and feeling. The master mind, however, can change his thought whenever he may so desire. A change of scene is not necessary because the master mind is not controlled by external conditions or circumstances. A change of scene will not produce a change of thought in his mind unless he so elects for the master mind changes his thoughts, ideas, or desires by imaging upon the mind the exact likeness of those new ideas, new thoughts, or new desires that have been selected.

The secret of the master mind is found wholly in the intelligent use of the imaging faculty, for man is as he thinks, and his thoughts are patterned after the predominating mental images, whether those images are impressions suggested from without or impressions formed by the mind through original thinking. When any individual permits his thoughts or desires to be formed in the likeness of impressions received from without he will be more or less controlled by environment. He will be largely in the hands of circumstances and fate, but when he proceeds to transform into an original idea every impression received from without and incorporates that idea into a new mental image he will use environment as a servant, thereby placing fate in his own hands.

Every object that is seen will produce an impression upon the mind according to the degree of mental susceptibility. This impression will contain the nature of the object of which it is a representation. Thus, the nature of that object will be reproduced in the mind, and what has thus entered the mind will be expressed more or less throughout the entire human system. Therefore, the individual who is susceptible to suggestions and external impressions will reproduce in his own mind and system conditions that are similar in nature to almost everything that he may see, hear or feel. He will, in consequence, be a reflection of the world in which he lives. He will think, speak and act as his surroundings may suggest. He will flow with the stream of his circumstances and he will be more or less of an automaton instead of a well individualized character.

However, every person who permits himself to be largely and continually affected by suggestions is more or less of an automaton, and accordingly is more or less in the hands of fate. So, therefore, in order to reverse matters and place fate in his own hands he must proceed to make intelligent use of suggestions instead of blindly following such desires and thoughts as his surroundings may suggest.

We are all surrounded constantly by suggestions of every description, because everything has the power to suggest something to us, provided we are susceptible. But there is a vast difference between permitting ourselves to be susceptible to all sorts of suggestions and by training ourselves to use intelligently all those impressions that suggestions may convey. The average student of suggestion not only ignores this difference, but encourages susceptibility to suggestion by constantly emphasizing the belief that it is suggestion that controls the world.

But if it is really true that suggestion does control the world, we want to learn how to so use suggestion that its indiscriminate control of the human mind may decrease steadily. For the human mind must not be controlled by anything, and this we can accomplish, not by teaching people how to use suggestion for the purpose of affecting their minds, but in using every impression conveyed by suggestion in the reconstruction of our own minds.

Suggestion is a part of life because everything has the power to suggest and all minds are open to impressions. Suggestion, therefore, is a necessary factor, and a permanent factor in our midst. But the problem is to train ourselves to make intelligent use of the impressions received, instead of blindly following the desires produced by such impressions, as the majority do.

To carry out this idea never permit the objects discerned by the senses to reproduce themselves in your mind against your will. Form your own ideas about what you see, hear or feel and try to make those ideas superior to what was suggested by the objects discerned. When you see evil do not form ideas or mental impressions that are similar to that evil. And do not think of the evil as bad, but try to understand the forces that are back of all evil, forces that are good in themselves though misdirected in their present state.

By trying to understand the nature that is back of evil or adversity you will not form bad ideas, and therefore will feel no bad effects from experiences that may seem undesirable. At the same time you will think your own thought about the experience, thereby developing the power of the master mind.

Surround yourself as far as possible with those things that suggest the superior, but do not permit such suggestions to determine your thought about the superior. The superior impressions that are suggested by superior environments should be used by yourself in forming still more superior thought. For if you wish to be a master mind your thought must always be higher than the thought your environment may suggest, no matter how ideal that environment may be.

Every impression that enters the mind through the senses should be worked out and should be made to serve the mind in its fullest capacity. In this way the original impression will not reproduce itself in the mind, but will become instrumental in giving the mind a number of new and superior ideas. To work out an impression try to see through its own nature ; that is, look at it from every conceivable point of view while trying to discern its causes, tendencies, possibilities and probable effects.

Use your imaging faculty in determining what you want to think or do, what you are to desire and what your tendencies are to be. Know what you want, then image those things upon the mind at all times. This will develop the power to think what you want to think. And he who can think what he wants to think can be what he wants to be. In this connection it is most important to realize that the principal reason why the average person has not realized his ideals is because he has not learned to think what he wants to think. He is too much affected by the suggestions that are all about him. He imitates his environment too much, following desires and tendencies that are not his own, and there- fore he is misled and misplaced.

Whenever you permit yourself to think what persons, things, conditions or circumstances may suggest, you are not thinking what you yourself want to think. You are following borrowed desires instead of your own desire. Therefore you will drift into strange thinking, thinking that is entirely different from what you have planned and that may; be directly opposed to your present purpose, need or ambition.

To obey the call of every suggestion and permit your mind to be carried away by this, that or the other, is to develop the tendency to drift ; your mind will wander, the power of concentration will weaken and you will become wholly incapable of really thinking what you want to think. In fact one line of constructive thinking will have scarcely begun when another line will be suggested, and you will leave the unfinished task to begin something else, which will in turn be left incomplete. Nothing, therefore, will be accomplished.

To become a master mind you must think what you want to think, no matter what your surroundings may suggest. And you must continue to think what you want to think until each particular purpose is carried out and every desired idea realized. Make it a point to desire what you want to desire and impress that desire so deeply upon consciousness that it cannot possibly be disturbed by such foreign desires as environment may suggest. Then continue to express that desire in all thought and action until you get what you want.

When you know that you have the right desire do not permit anything to influence your mind to change. Take such influences and suggestions and convert them into the desire that you have already decided upon, thereby giving that desire additional life and power. However, you should never close your mind to impressions from without. Try to gain valuable impressions from every source, but do not follow those impressions. Use them in building up your own system of original thought. Then think what you want to think under every circumstance and so use every impression you receive that you will gain still greater power to think what you want to think. Thus you will readily and surely develop the master mind.

CHAPTER XV.

THE POWER OF MIND OVER BODY.

It is through the law of vibration that the mind exercises its power over the body. And through this law every action of the mind produces a chemical effect in the body, that is, an effect that actually takes place in the substance of the physical form. The process of this law is readily understood when we find that every mental action is a vibration, and passes through every atom in the body, modifying both the general conditions and the chemical conditions of every group of cells.

A chemical change in the body is produced by a change in the vibrations of the different elements of the body because every element is what it is by virtue of the rate of vibrations of its atoms. Everything in the universe is what it is because of its rate of vibration ; therefore, anything may be changed in nature and quality by changing the rate of its vibrations.

When we change the vibrations of ice it becomes water. When we change the vibrations of water it becomes steam. When we change the vibrations of ordinary earth in one or more ways it becomes green grass, roses, trees or waving fields of grain, depending upon the changes that are made. Nature is constantly changing the vibrations of her elements thus producing all sorts of forms, colors and appearances. In fact, the vast panorama of nature, both that which is visible to the senses and that which is not all is produced by constant changes in the vibrations of the elements and forces of nature.

Man, however, is doing the same in his kingdom, that is, in mind and personality. We all are changing the vibrations of different parts of our system every second, though all such changes are, of course, produced within the bounds of natural law. We know that by exercising the power of thought in any form or manner we can produce the vibrations both of our states of mind and our physical conditions. And when we exercise this power to the fullest degree possible we can change the vibrations of everything in our system and thus produce practically any condition that may be desired. This gives us a power that is extraordinary to say the least. But it is not a power that we have to secure. We have it already and we employ it every minute, because to think is to exercise this power. This being true the problem is to use this power intelligently and thus not only secure desirable results, or results as desired, but also to secure superior results to anything we have secured before.

When we analyze this law of vibration we find that every unpleasant condition that man has felt in his body has come from a false change in the vibrations of some of the elements in his body. And we also find that every agreeable condition has come from a true change in those vibrations, that is, a change towards the better. Here we should remember that every change in the vibrations of the human system that takes us down, so to speak into the lesser grade is a false change and will produce unnatural or detrimental effects, while every change that is an ascending change in the scale is beneficial.

To apply this law intelligently it is necessary to know what chemical changes each particular mental action has the power to produce, and also how we may so regulate mental actions that all changes in the vibrations of our system may be changes along the line of the ascending scale. This, however, leads us into a vast and most fascinating subject; but on account of its vastness we can only mention it here, which is all that is necessary in this connection, as our object for the present is simply to give the reason why every mental action produces a chemical change in the body.

Since every element in the body is what it is because it vibrates at a certain rate ; since every mental action is a vibration; since every vibration that comes from an inner plane can modify vibrations that act upon an outer plane; and since all vibrations are within the physical plane of action, we understand perfectly why every mental action will tend to produce a chemical change in the body. Although it is also true that two different grades of vibration on the same plane, or in the same sphere of action, may modify each other, still they do so only when the one is much stronger than the other.

All mental vibrations act more deeply in chemical life than the physical vibrations; therefore the former can entirely change the latter, no matter how strong the latter may seem to be. And this is how the mind exercises power over the body. Some mental vibrations, however, are almost as near to the surface as the physical ones and for that reason produce but slight changes, changes that are some times imperceptible. Knowing this we understand why the power of mind over body becomes greater in proportion to the depth of consciousness and feeling that we enter into during any process of thought.

Therefore when we promote such changes in the body as we may desire or decide upon we must cultivate deeper consciousness, or what may be called subjective consciousness. This is extremely important because we can eliminate practically any physical disease or undesired physical condition by producing the necessary chemical change in those physical elements where that particular condition resides at the time. This is how medicine aims to cure and it does cure whenever it produces the necessary chemical change. But it fails so frequently in this respect that it cannot be depended upon under all circumstances.

Mental vibrations, however, when deep or subjective can in every case produce the necessary chemical change in the elements concerned. And the desired vibrations are invariably produced by positive, constructive and wholesome mental actions, provided those actions are deeply felt. Thus we realize that the power of mind acting through the law of vibration can, by changing or modifying the vibrations of the different elements in the body, produce almost any change desired in the physical conditions of the body.

What we wish to emphasize in this connection are the facts that every mental action is a vibration; that it permeates every atom of the body; that it comes up from the deeper chemical life, thereby working beneath the elements and forces of the physical body ; and that according to a chemical law can modify and change the vibrations of those elements and forces to almost any extent within the sphere of natural law.

To modify the vibrations of the physical elements is to produce a chemical change in the body. But whether this change will be desirable or undesirable depends upon the nature of the mental action that produces the change. Therefore by entertaining and perpetuating only such mental actions as tend to produce desirable changes, or the changes we want in the body, we can secure practically any physical change desired ; and we may thereby exercise the power of mind over body to an extent that will have practically no limitation within the natural workings of the human domain.

CHAPTER XVI.

THE POWER OF MIND OVER DESTINY.

The destiny of every individual is being created hourly by himself, and that something that determines what he is to create at any particular period in time is the sum total of his ideals. The future of the person is not preordained by some external power, nor is fate controlled by some strange and mysterious force that master minds can alone comprehend and apply. It is our ideals that control and determine our fate. And we all have our ideals, whether we be aware of the fact or not.

To have ideals is not simply to have dreams or visions of that which lies beyond the attainment of the person, nor is idealism a system of ideas that the practical mind would not have the privilege to entertain. To have ideals is to have definite objects in view, be those objects very high, very low or anywhere between those extremes. The ideals of any mind are simply the wants, the desires and the aims of that mind, and as every normal mind will invariably live, think and work for that which is wanted by his present state of existence, it is evident that every mind must necessarily follow his ideals both consciously and unconsciously.

However, when those ideals are low or inferior the individual will naturally work for the ordinary and the inferior, and the products of his mind will correspond in quality to that for which he is working. Thus inferior causes will spring up everywhere in his life and inferior effects will inevitably follow. But when those ideals are high and superior he will work for the superior ; he will develop superiority in himself and he will give superiority to everything that he may produce. Accordingly every action that he originates in his life will become a superior cause and will be followed by a superior effect.

The destiny of every individual is determined by what he is and by what he is doing. And what any individual is to be or do is determined by what he is living for, thinking for, or working for, be those objects great or small, superior or inferior. Man is not being made by some outside force, nor is the fate of man the result of causes outside of himself. Man is making himself as well as his future with what he is working for and in all his efforts he invariably follows his ideals.

It is therefore evident that he who lives, thinks and works for the superior becomes superior while he who works for less becomes less. And also that any individual may become more, achieve more, secure more and create for himself a better future and a greater destiny by beginning to think, live and work for a superior group of ideals.

To have low ideals is to give the creative forces of the system something ordinary to work for. To have high ideals is to give those forces something extraordinary to work for. And the fate of man is the result of what those forces are constantly producing. Every force in the human system is producing something and that something will become a part both of the individual and his external circumstances.

It is therefore evident that any individual can improve the power, the quality and the worth of his being by directing the forces of his system to produce something that has quality and worth. Those forces, however, are not directed or controlled entirely by the will, because it is their nature to produce what the mind desires, wants or needs. And the desires of any mind are determined directly by the leading ideals entertained in that mind.

The forces of the system will begin to work for the superior when the mind begins to entertain superior ideals. And since it is the product of those creative forces that determine both the nature and the destiny of man it is evident that a superior nature and a greater destiny may be secured by any individual who will adopt, and live up to, the highest and the most perfect system of idealism that he can possibly comprehend.

To entertain superior ideals is to picture in the mind, and to hold constantly before the mind, the highest conceptions that can be formed of everything of which we may be conscious. To dwell mentally in those higher conceptions at all times is to cause the predominating ideals to become superior ideals. And it is the ruling ideals for which we live, think and work.

When the ruling ideals of any mind are superior the creative forces of that mind will produce the superior in every element, faculty, talent or power in that mind. Thus the greater will be developed in that mind, and the great mind invariably creates a better future and a greater destiny.

To entertain superior ideals is not to dream of the impossible, but to enter into mental contact with those greater possibilities that we are not able to discern. And to have the power to discern an ideal indicates that we have the power to realize that ideal. For the fact is we do not become conscious of greater possibilities until we have developed sufficient capacity to work out those possibilities into practical tangible results.

Therefore when we discern the greater we are ready to attain and achieve the greater, but before we can proceed to do what we are ready to do we must adopt superior ideals, and live up to those ideals according to our full capacity and power. When our ideals are superior we shall think constantly of the superior because as our ideals are, so is our thinking. And to thing constantly of the superior is to grow steadily into the likeness of the superior. Thus all the forces of the mind will move toward the superior. All things in the life of the individual will work together with greater and greater goals in view, and continuous advancement on a larger and broader scale must inevitably follow.

To entertain superior ideals is not simply to desire some larger personal attainment, nor is it to dwell mentally in some belief that is different from the usual beliefs of the world. To entertain superior ideals is simply to think the best thought about everything and to try to improve upon that thought every day. Superior idealism therefore is not mere dreaming of the great and beautiful. It is also the actual living in mental harmony with the very best we know in all things, in all persons, in all circumstances and in all expressions of life. To live in mental harmony with the best we can find anywhere is to create the best in our own mentalities and personalities.

And as we grow steadily into the likeness of that which we think of the most we will in this manner increase our power, capacity and worth, and in consequence be able to create a better future and a more worthy destiny. For it is the law under every circumstance that the man who becomes much will achieve much, and great attainments are invariably followed by a greater future.

To think of anything that is less than the best or to dwell mentally with the inferior is to neutralize the effect of those superior ideals that we have begun to entertain. It is therefore absolutely necessary to entertain superior ideals only, and to cease all recognition of inferiority or imperfection if we want to secure the best results along these lines.

In this connection we find the reason why the majority fail to secure any tangible results from higher ideals, for the fact is they entertain too many lower ideals at the same time. They may aim high, they may adore the beautiful, they may desire the perfect, they may live for the better and they may work for the greater, but they do not think their best thoughts about everything; therefore the house in their case is divided against itself and cannot stand.

Superior idealism, however, contains no thought that is less than the best, and it entertains no desire that has not greater worth in view. Such idealism does not recognize the power of evil in anything or in anybody. It may know that adverse conditions do exist, but it gives the matter no conscious thought whatever. And to pursue this course is absolutely necessary if we would create a better future. For it is not possible to think the best thought about everything while the mind gives conscious attention to adversity and imperfection.

The true idealist therefore gives conscious recognition only to the power of good. And he lives in the conviction that all things in his life are working together for good. But this conviction is not mere sentiment with him because he knows that all things will work together for good when we recognize only the good, think only the good, desire only the good, expect only the good and live only for the good.

To apply the principle of superior idealism in all things, that is, to live, think and work only for the highest ideals that we can comprehend means advancement in all things. To follow the superior ideal is to move towards the higher, the greater and the superior. And no one can continue very long in that mode of living, thinking and acting without creating for himself a new world, a better environment and a fairer destiny.

We understand therefore that in order to create a better future we must begin now to select a better group of ideals, for it is our ideals that constitute the cause of the future we expect to create. And as the cause is so will also be the effect.

CHAPTER XVII.

THE X-RAY POWER OF THE MIND.

There are many things that the human mind can do and all of them are remarkable when viewed from the highest pinnacle of consciousness but one of the greatest and most wonderful is the power of mind to see through things ; that is, to cause the rays of its insight and discernment to pass through the problems of life just as the X-ray passes through opaque and tangible substances. This power is latent in every mind and is active to a considerable degree in many minds ; and on account of the extreme value of this power its development should be promoted in every possible manner.

When this power is highly developed practically all mistakes can be avoided. The right thing can be done at the right time, and every opportunity can be taken advantage of when the psychological moment is at hand; and in addition that finer perception of life will be gained through which consciousness may expand into larger and larger fields until the mind goes beyond all limitations and lives in the spirit of the universal.

We are all surrounded by possibilities that can never be measured, possibilities which, if employed even in a limited degree, would make life many times as rich and beautiful as it is now. The average person, however, does not see these many larger and greater ways of adding to the value and worth of existence. In other words, he cannot see through the circumstances of his life and thus take possession of the more substantial elements of growth, attainment and realization. Therefore life with him continues to remain a very ordinary matter.

He may know that there are better things in store and that there is something just beyond his present conception of life that could change his life completely if he could only lay hold upon it ; still here is where he fails. He is in the dark. He cannot see how to proceed in gaining those greater and better things that life must contain. There is something in the way of his vision, a cloud, a veil, or an obstacle of some kind that hides the path to better things. And he cannot see through the obstacle. For this reason he remains where he is, wondering why he has not the power to reach what he is absolutely certain could be reached.

Millions of minds complain "if we could only have things cleared up." This is the problem everywhere. Therefore, if they could all see their way clear what might they not accomplish both for themselves and others. But as a rule they do not see their way clear. Occasional glimpses of light appear when the real path to all good things seems to reveal itself, but before they are ready to take this path another cloud comes in the way and they have no idea what to do next. This is the experience of the average person along these lines.

And there seems to be no hope for the average person of ever passing from the lesser to the greater. The reason seems to be that when everything looks bright and the way is clear for greater results, desirable changes, more happiness and a larger life, something invariably happens to confuse things again, and the way to pastures green has for the time being been closed up once more. However, there is a way out of all sorts of conditions and everybody can find this way. Though it is a fact well to remember that every individual must always see this way for himself.

To proceed, everybody must develop the power to see through things. In fact, see through all things, or in other words, learn to use the X-ray of what may be termed superior degrees of intelligence. Every mind has this X-ray, this higher power to penetrate and see through the difficult and the confused. And there is no condition, no circumstance, no obstacle, no mystery through which this ray cannot penetrate. Therefore, when we employ this X-ray of the mind we clear up everything, we see exactly where we are going, where we ought to go and where we should not go. So that to live constantly in the light of these finer grades of intelligence is to live in the cleared up atmosphere perpetually, no matter where our sphere of activity may be.

That those minds who live in the lower atmosphere of thought cannot see clearly where they are going is quite natural. Because in the first place these lower atmospheres of life are usually dense, being surcharged with the confused thought of the world; and in the second place, those who live in these lower grades do not employ the higher and finer rays of mental light.

We all know that the lower vibrations of physical light cannot pass through objects that are opaque. And we have also learned that the lower rays of mental light cannot pass through conditions and circumstances that are confused with discord and materiality. But it has been demonstrated that the higher rays of physical light can pass through almost any physical object. In like manner the higher rays of intelligence or mental light can see through almost anything in the mental world. And, therefore, the one who employs these higher rays of his mind will have the power to see through all things in his life.

However, when we speak of higher grades of intelligence as being the power that can see through things we must not infer that such intelligence is too high to be gained by the average individual. For the fact is that we all have this higher intelligence or finer rays of mental light active within us at all times. The secret is simply to learn how to apply these finer rays of mental light ; thus we shall all be able to exercise the power to see through things.

The difference between the lower and the higher rays of light is found almost wholly in the attitude of the mind. That is, it is materiality on the one hand and spirituality on the other hand. By materiality we mean the attitude of mind that looks down ; an attitude that is absorbed wholly in things ; that dwells on the surface, and that lives exclusively for the body, not being consciously interested in anything but the body.

By spirituality we mean that attitude of the mind that gives an upward look to every thought, every desire, every motive, every feeling and every action of the entire being of man. But this upward look is not an attitude that looks for the invisible, nor an attitude that dreams of the glories of another sphere of existence. It is an attitude that simply looks for the greater possibilities that exist everywhere now, and for the beauty and the truth that crowns the whole world.

The mind that is material or that lives exclusively in the world of things is more or less in the clouds of confusion, therefore employs the lesser rays of intelligence, those rays that do not have the power to see through things. Such a mind, therefore, can never be in a cleared-up mental atmosphere. At times those minds that have been conscious of higher grades of mentality and that have seen the superiority and the brilliancy of this higher intelligence within them, may fall down temporarily into materiality, and for the time being they may lose sight completely of the higher consciousness of truth which they previously gained. Thus they frequently forget every principle in higher experience that once was so vivid, and while in this state of depression they generally conclude that all is sin, sorrow and human weakness after all; that is, it seems so to such a mind, because at such a time it is only the discord of the world and the results of mistakes that are discerned.

While in this submerged state the mind cannot see the splendors that are immediately beyond, and he cannot feel the supreme joy that higher realms have in store. Accordingly he comes to the conclusion that all is trouble and pain ; he feels nothing else, knows nothing else and has temporarily forgotten the light and the joy that he knew while in higher realms of consciousness. The wise man who wrote the proverbs was in this lower mentality when he declared that all is vanity and vexation of spirit. And he spoke the truth about that lower world, that is, that material state that is composed wholly of the mistakes of man.

That material state, however, is not the only world that there is. There are other and finer worlds in the mind of man worlds where vanity does not exist and where nothing vexes the spirit. It is these higher and finer worlds of the mind that we must train ourselves to love, if we wish to see through things and thus learn to understand things as they really are. Then we shall find that the wrong is insignificant compared with the immensity of the right and the good.

When we look at things from a worldly or materialistic point of view, things do not appear very well, nor are things always very well in that particular state. They are frequently wrong and misdirected. But when we learn to see through things and see all things as they are we change our minds. Then we discover other worlds and other and higher stories to the mansion in which we live. The cellar is usually dark and damp, but how much better we find it further up. And yet when the average person is in the cellar of his mind he imagines that it is the only place there is and that there is neither light, comfort nor joy in the world. But why should we ever enter the cellar of the mind, and why should we permit a dark damp cellar to exist in our minds at all? There is no need of it in human life, for it is simply the sum total of our mistakes, and does not represent the real mansion of existence in any sense of the term.

The whole of the being of man should be illumined and every atom should be filled with harmony, comfort, joy and life. When the mind that had fallen down comes up again it realizes how absurd it was to forget all the truth and all the joy of real existence simply because there were a few clouds for a little time. However, after a few such experiences the mind learns to interpret the experience of the cellar and does not consider it real any more, but on the contrary makes haste to prevent that experience as well as all other descending attitudes in the future.

The mind that has never experienced the higher phases of consciousness does not know how to proceed to prevent the more adverse experiences of ordinary existence, and therefore will remain among the dense fogs of confusion more or less until taught how to rise into the finer grades of mental light. To proceed in rising above these undesirable conditions the first step to take is to make harmony, happiness and brightness of spirit the great objects in view. Even when we simply think of these states we elevate the mind in a measure, and whenever the mind is elevated to some extent we find that finer light comes into our world of intelligence; that is, the higher rays of mentality begin to express themselves and many things begin to clear up.

In this connection it is well to remember that our brightest ideas come while we are on the mountain top of intellectual activity, and also that we can find the correct answer to almost any problem that may appear in personal life if we only go up in mind as high as we possibly can reach at the time. While the mind is up in those finer grades of intellect the most abstract principles are comprehended with almost no mental effort, and the path to greater things becomes as clear as the midday sun.

It is therefore a great and valuable accomplishment to be able to go up in the mind as high as one may wish. For to bring superior intelligence into constant use is to live in the world of absolute light itself, the reason being that this intelligence actually does possess X-ray power of penetration in the mental world. ' There is nothing that this ray cannot see through, and there nothing is hidden that it cannot reveal to light.

Again we must remember, however, that it is not necessary to attain an enormous amount of wisdom and knowledge in order to gain the power to see through things in this way, because every stage of development that exists has the power to see through everything that may appear in that particular stage. Every individual in his present state has the power to see through everything in that state, that is, a finer grade of a mental light that belongs to that particular state and it has the X-ray power of penetration in its own sphere. Accordingly he can learn to see through everything where he is without becoming a mental giant, or without acquiring wisdom which belongs exclusively to higher states of mental attainment.

The idea is to live in the upper story of your mental world whatever that world may be now, because by entering the upper story of your mental world you enter that state of your present intelligence that can see through everything that pertains to your present world. In order to enter the upper story of the mind the whole of life should be concentrated so to speak, upon the most superior states of existence that we can conceive of. This will cause the mind to become ascending in its attitude and the power of the ascending mind is immense. Such a mind will steadily grow upward and onward towards higher and finer grades of intellect, wisdom and mental light, and gradually this power to see through things will be gained. In addition everything will be turned to greater use and better use, and thus be made more conducive to a life of beauty, richness and joy.

However, when we proceed to consecrate a life to the superior in this manner we do not leave the world of things. We simply turn the life and the power of all things towards the higher, the larger and the better. We thereby cause the world of things to move steadily towards superior states of life and action. As we enter more and more into this upper realm of thought, light and understanding we should employ this penetrating power of finer intelligence in connection with every move we make. For it is the constant use and the true use of a power that develops that power. Therefore, we should do nothing without first turning on the X--ray of the mind. In other words, we should view every circumstance from the standpoint of a clearer perception before any decision is made, and we should seek to secure the very highest viewpoint under every circumstance. This will not only give the mind a better understanding of how to proceed, but the faculty of finer discernment will be developed constantly, and our growth in wisdom and intellectual brilliancy will in time become remarkable.

In this connection we should remember that nearly all the missteps that are taken in the average life are the results of the mind's failure to penetrate the surface of things and conditions so as to see the real nature of the factors at work. But the lower mental rays, that is, that phase of intelligence that we use while in the lower story of the mind, do not possess this penetrating power. Therefore, if we learn to live, think and act correctly under all sorts of circumstances we must learn to employ the X-ray of the mind; that is, that light of the mind that we are conscious of when living in the upper story of the mind ; and it is when we are in that light that we can see through all things.

CHAPTER XVIII.

WHEN MIND IS BROAD AND DEEP.

It has become a virtue to be broad minded, but there are times when certain virtues become so extreme in their actions that they cease to contain any virtue. In like manner it is possible for the mind to become so broad that it contains practically nothing of value being too superficial in its effort to cover the whole field to possess a single idea of merit.

To be progressive in thought is another admirable trait in the eyes of the modern world, but there are not a few of our advanced thinkers who advance so rapidly, according to their own conception of advancement, that their own minds are literally left behind; that is, they become so absorbed in the act of moving forward that no attention is given to that power that alone can produce advancement. In consequence their remarkable progress is in the imagination only.

Here it is well to remember that all is not thought that comes from the mind or that is produced in the mind. For the mere fact that we are thinking does not prove that we are creating thought. A large percentage of the products of the average mind is but heaps of intellectual debris accumulated in one place today and moved to another place in the mind tomorrow. In brief, too much of our modern thinking is simply a moving of useless mental material from one side of consciousness to another. However, in promoting the right use of the mind this practice is something that must be avoided absolutely for the mind cannot work to advantage under such conditions.

Thought that really is thought is the product of design and purpose, and is invariably the result of systematic efforts to work out principles. Accordingly such thought contains the power to serve certain definite objects in view. We should therefore realize that no product of the mind constitutes real thought unless it is the result of designed thinking and is created for a certain special purpose. A pile of brick is not a house, but a house may be built from those bricks if they are arranged according to special design and put together for a definite purpose.

The broad mind should endeavor to embrace much, but should not attempt to hold more than can be applied practically and thoroughly and according to the purpose which it is desired to fulfill. In other words, the object is not to see how much we can hold in the mind, but how much we can actually possess or use; not how much ground we can cover, but how much we can take care of in the best manner, and cultivate scientifically.

In this connection it is most important to understand that the mind that becomes broad enough to accept everything will also accept the illusions, the vagaries and the foundationless theories that are so numerous everywhere. There are a number of people today who do this very thing and call themselves liberal, advanced, charitable and broadly progressive. But the fact is that their minds constitute a hopeless mixture of truths, half truths and illusions. Accordingly they accomplish very little, and what is more serious they confuse the beginners in genuine advanced thought and thus tend to place the real truth of our progressive movements in a false light.

However, there is a progress that is progressive, There is an advancement that actually does advance and we have much of it today. But there are many movements and many people claiming to be broad who are broad only in the sense of keeping the mental doors wide open to everything that may desire to come in. But such broad mindedness must be avoided at every turn because it tends to make the mind shallow, superficial and inefficient, thereby rendering the mentality incapable of actually taking possession of a single genuine idea or mental power.

The mind that is broad in the true sense of the term does not try to embrace everything, but tries to penetrate everything. Its object is not to simply take in and hold, but to enter into and understand and thereby gain real control and possession of facts, talents and powers. The truth is that to be broad minded is not to be ready to believe everything, but to be ready to examine everything, and to accept everything that proves itself true regardless of how it may conflict with objects, views or opinions.

A broad mind never takes things on authority, but is eternally in search of the one authority truth that is back of and within all things.

In brief, to be able to see the true side of every belief, every system, every idea and every experience this is genuine broad mindedness.

In considering this subject we must remember that what we accept becomes a part of ourselves. Therefore it is a most serious mistake to take into the mind everything that may come along. The fact is we cannot possibly exercise too much care in selecting our ideas, although we must not go to the other extreme and become so particular that we remain dissatisfied with everything. There is a happy medium in this connection that everyone can establish by training the mind to penetrate everything for the purpose of understanding the principles that underlie everything.

It has been well stated that we gradually grow into the likeness of that which we admire the most and think of the most. And it is true that we nearly always have special admiration for that which we constantly defend, whether we have fully accepted the same as true or not. The mind that is willing to accept almost anything for the sake of being broad will also be ready to defend almost anything to justify that position. Therefore to defend all theories the past has advanced, is to reproduce our minds more or less in the likeness of all those theories. But since those theories contradict each other at almost every turn, many of them being illusions, we can readily imagine the result. In fact, the mind will, under such circumstances, be divided against itself and will be incapable of doing its work according to principle and law.

A confused mind is the greatest obstacle to real progress and the attempt to take in every new idea as true because it is new will invariably confuse the mind, and what is more such a practice will so derange judgment that after a while the mind will not be able to discriminate intelligently between the right and the wrong in any sphere of life.

In this connection we must remember that among the new ideas that are springing up in the world the larger number are either half truths or illusions. And the reason why so many of these ideas are accepted as true is because real broad mindedness, that is, that attitude of mind that does not embrace everything but attempts to penetrate everything, is an art yet to be acquired by the majority. The average mind is ready to take in and hold almost any belief or idea if it happens to produce an impression that is favorable to his present condition of life, but there are few who are training their minds to penetrate everything for the purpose of understanding everything. For this reason a mass of ideas are accepted that contain neither virtue, truth nor power.

The attitude of tolerance is closely connected with broad mindedness and is usually considered an exceptional virtue. But again we are liable to be misled because there are two kinds of tolerance; the one holds a passive charity for everything without trying to find out the truth about anything; while the other enters into friendly relation with all things in order that the good and true that may exist in those things can be found.

The attitude of tolerance, however, is always valuable, in so far as it eliminates the spirit of criticism, because the spirit of criticism can never find the truth. But the spirit of friendly research always does find the truth. For this reason the penetrating mind must be kind, gentle and sympathetic. If it is not, the very elements that are to be examined will be scattered and misplaced. Besides it is the substance of things that contains the truth, and to enter into this substance the mind must be in sympathetic touch with the life and the soul of that which it seeks to understand.

That attitude of tolerance that is passive, is either indifferent, or will soon become indifferent; and mental indifference leads to stagnation, which in turn makes the mind so inactive that it is completely controlled by every condition or environment with which it may come in contact. Such a tolerance, therefore, must be avoided and avoided absolutely.

True tolerance refrains from criticism at all times but that is only one side of its nature. The other side enters into the closest mental contact \with all things and penetrates to the very depths of the principles upon which these things are based. In this way the mind readily discovers those ideas and beliefs that constitute the true expressions of principles, and also discovers those which are mere perversions. However, the tolerant mind does not condemn the perversions. It forgets them entirely by giving added life and attention to the true expressions , and thereby proceeds to give lull and positive action to all those ideas and powers of which it has gained possession by being broad as well as deep.

CHAPTER XIX.

THE GREATEST MIND OF ALL.

In order that we may rise in the scale of life the mind must fix attention upon the ideal. And the ideal may be defined as that possible something that is above and beyond present realization. To become more and accomplish more we must transcend the lesser and enter the greater. But there can be no transcending action unless there is a higher goal toward which all the elements within us are moving; and there can be no higher goal unless there is a clear discernment of the ideal.

The more distinctly the mind discerns the ideal, and the more frequently the ideal is brought directly before the actions of attention the more will the mind think of the ideal; and the mind invariably moves towards that which we think of the most. The man with no ideals will think constantly that which is beneath the ideal, or rather that which is the opposite of the ideal ; that is, he will think the most of that which is low, inferior and unworthy. In consequence he will drift more and more into the life of nothingness, emptiness, inferiority and want. Tie will steadily go down into the lesser until he wants for everything, both on the mental and physical planes.

The man, however, who has high ideals will think the most of the greater things in life, and accordingly will advance perpetually into the possession of everything that has greatness, superiority and high worth. The wise men of the past declared that the nation with no visions would perish. And the cause of this fact is simple. When we are not going up we are going down. To live is to be in action and there is no standstill in action. To continue to go down is to finally perish. Therefore to prevent such an end we must continue to go up. But we cannot continue to go up towards the higher unless we have constant visions of the higher. We cannot move mentally or physically towards that which we do not see. Nor can we desire that of which we have never been conscious.

In like manner the individual who has no ideals and no visions of greater things will continue to go down until his life becomes mere emptiness. Thus everything in his nature that has worth will perish, and finally he will have nothing to live for. When he discovers himself he will find that there are but two courses to pursue: To continue to live in the vale of tears he has made for himself ; or to ascend towards the heights of emancipation, those heights which can be reached only by following the lofty vision.

It is the visions of greater things that arouse the mind to greater action. It is higher ideals that inspire man to create more nobly in the real, and it is the touch of things sublime that awakens in human nature that beautiful something that makes life truly worth living. Without ideals no person will ever attain greatness, neither will there be any improvement in the world. But every person who has ideals, and who lives to realize his ideals, will positively attain greatness, and will positively improve everything, both in his life and in his environment.

It must be clearly evident to all minds who understand the true functions of the ideal that the life of man will be worthless unless inspired by the ideal, and also that everything that is worth while in human existence comes directly from man's effort to rise towards the ideal. Such men, therefore, who are constantly placing high ideals before the world in a manner that will attract the attention of the World it is such men who invariably have the greatest mind of all.

The majority have not the power to discern the ideal clearly without having their attention aroused by the vivid description of some lucid mind that already does see the ideal. But when their attention is aroused and the ideal is made clear to their minds, they will begin at once to rise in the scale. That individual, therefore, who is constantly placing ideals before the minds of the many is causing the many to rise towards the more worthy and the more beautiful in life. In consequence he is not only doing great things himself, but he is causing thousands of others to do great things. He is not only awakening the superior powers in his own nature, but he is also awakening those powers in the natures of vast multitudes. His mind, therefore, is doing work that is great indeed.

However, to place ideals before the minds of others, it is not necessary to make that particular purpose a profession, nor is it sufficient to reveal idealism in the mere form of written or spoken words. Actions speak louder than words and the man who does things exercises a far greater power for good than the man who simply says things. The ideal can be made a vital and a ruling element in every vocation. And all men and women can reveal the ideal through their work without giving voice to a single word concerning any particular system of idealism.

But it is not necessary to be silent concerning those sublime visions that daily appear before the mind, although it is well to remember that we always secure the best results when we do a great deal more than we say. The man who makes his work an inspiration to greater things will invariably do greater and greater work and he will also cause thousands of others to do greater work. He will make his own ideals practical and tangible, and will thereby make the ideal intelligible to the majority. For though it is true that great words inspire the few, it requires great deeds to inspire the many.

The man who makes his own life worth while will cause thousands of others to make their lives worth while. In consequence the value and happiness that he will add to the sum total of human existence cannot possibly be measured. He is placing great and living ideals before the world and must therefore be counted among those who possess the greatest mind in the world. The man who performs a great work has achieved greatness, but his work is the work of one man only. That man, however, who places high ideals before the minds of the many, thereby awakening the greatness that is latent within the many, causes a greater work to be performed by each one of the many; thus he gives origin to a thousand great deeds, where the former gives origin to a few only. That he is greater in exact proportion is therefore a fact that cannot be disputed. For this reason we must conclude that the greatest mind of all is invariably that mind that can inspire the greatest number to live, think and work for the vision.

To awaken the greatness that is latent in man is to awaken the cause of everything that has real worth in the world. Such work, therefore, is the greatest of all great work and it is a work that lies within the power of everybody. For we all can awaken the greatness that is latent in other minds by placing high ideals before those minds.

The great soul lives in the world of superior visions and aims to make those visions real by training all the powers of mind and personality to move towards those visions. And here it is highly important to realize that when the powers of mind and personality steadily move towards the ideal they will create the ideal more and more in the present, thereby making the ideal real in the present.

To live where there is neither improvement nor advancement is to live a life that is utterly worthless. But improvement and advancement are not possible without ideals. We must have visions of the better before we can make things better. And before we can make things better we must discern the greater before we can rise out of the lesser. To advance is to move towards something that is beyond the present; but there can be no advancement until that something is discerned. And as everything that is beyond the present is ideal, the mind must necessarily have idealism before any advancement can possibly take place.

Everything that is added to the value of life has been produced because some one had ideals ; because some one revealed those ideals; and because some one tried to make those ideals real. It is therefore evident that when lofty ideals are constantly placed before the mind of the whole world we may add immeasurably to the value of life, and in every manner conceivable.

The same law through which we may increase that which is desired in life we may apply for the elimination of that which is not desired. And to remove what is not desired the secret is to press on towards the ideal. The ideal contains what is desired, and to enter that which is desired is to rise out of that which is not desired. Through the application of this law we eliminate the usual method of resistance, which is highly important, because when we antagonize the wrong or that which is not desired we give life to the wrong, thereby adding to its power. For the fact is we always give power to that which we resist or antagonize. In consequence we will, through such a method, either perpetuate the wrong or remove one wrong by placing another in its stead.

However, no wrong was ever righted in the world until the race ignored that wrong and began to rise into the corresponding right. And to enter into this rising attitude is to become an idealist. It is not the iconoclast, but the idealist who reforms the world. And the greatest reformer is invariably that man whose conception of the ideal is so clear that his entire mind is illumined by a brilliant light of superior worlds. His thought, his life, his word, his action in brief, everything connected with his existence, gives the same vivid description of the ideal made real. And every person with whom he may come in contact will be inspired to live on those same superior heights of sublime existence.

When we try to force any ill away from any part of the system, be the system that of an individual, a community, or a race, we invariably cause a similar or modified ill to appear in some other part of that system. For the fact is that no ill can be eliminated until it is replaced by wholeness. And wholeness will not enter the system until the system enters wholeness. We must enter the light before we can receive or possess the light. And to enter wholeness is to enter the ideal and perfect existence.

To enter the ideal, however, it is necessary to understand the ideal. Every form of emancipation as well as every process of advancement will depend directly upon the mind's understanding of the ideal, and its aspiration towards the ideal. A strong ascending desire to realize the ideal will in the life of any individual cause the entire system of that individual to outgrow everything that is inferior or undesirable. In consequence complete emancipation and greater and greater attainments must invariably follow.

When we understand this subject thoroughly we realize that if all the strong minds in the world would constantly face the idea!, giving all their power to the attainment of the ideal and living completely in the reality of the ideal, a live current permeating the whole race would begin to move towards the ideal. And so strong would this current become that its power would be irresistible. The natural result would be that the ideal would be realized more and more in every individual life of the race. This possibility demonstrates the extreme value of the ideal and the importance of living absolutely for the ideal. It also demonstrates the fact that all such men and women who are constantly placing the ideal before the minds of the world possess the greatest minds in the world. For it is only such minds that can inspire the masses of minds to discern the ideal, to desire the ideal and to live for the realization of the ideal.

CHAPTER XX.

WHEN MIND IS ON THE HEIGHTS.

When the great soul transcends the world of things it invariably begins to dream of that which is greater, finer, more perfect, more beautiful and more sublime than what the life of present experience has been able to produce. But those dreams are not mere dreams ; they are actually glimpses of what is possible or what may be near at hand ; that is, prophetic visions of what is to be. The dreams of the small soul are usually temporary creations of an unguided imagination. But the dreams of the great soul are flashes of light emanating from the realms of supreme light, revealing secrets that man shall some day be able to make his own.

What the great soul discerns in his visions and dreams is nothing less than that greater life and those greater things into the possession of which he is being prepared to enter. But if we would gain those greater things which are in store we must proceed to claim our own, and not simply continue to dream. The prophetic vision of the great soul does not reveal what will come to pass of its own accord, but what such a soul is now competent to bring to pass, provided he will use the powers that are in his possession now. In brief, a prophetic vision does not reveal something that is coming to you, but reveals something that you now have the power to bring to yourself if you will.

The soul that can transcend the world of passing things and dream of the world of better things is now in possession of the necessary power to make his dreams come true. For the fact is, we cannot discern the ideal until we have the power to make it real, nor can the mind arise into worlds sublime until it has gained the power to make its own life sublime. Therefore the soul that can look into the mystic future and discern a more beautiful life is prepared for such a life, has found the secret path to such a life, has the power to create such a life, though not merely in ages to come, but now. For what we see in our visions today we have the power to bring to pass in the present.

This is indeed a great truth, and than this, nothing could possibly bring greater joy to the soul of man.

If we can see better days while our minds are on the heights we can rest assured that we have the power to create better days. But we must proceed to use that power if we would enter into the pastures green that are before us. The law is that what we see in the ideal we must work for in the actual, for it is in this way alone that our dreams can come true without fail.

The dreams of the great soul always appear when the mind is on the heights. And it is such dreams alone that can contain the prophetic vision. What we dream of while on the low lands of life has no value. The fact is that if we would know the next step ; if we would know what today can bring forth ; if we would know what is best now; if we would know what we are able to attain and achieve now ; if we would know those greater things that are now in store for us, we must rise to the mountain top of the soul's transcendent existence. It is there, and there alone, that these things are made known. And every mind can at times ascend to those sublime heights. The great soul can readily rise to these mountain tops ; in brief, such a soul has no other visions than those that appear on the mountain tops. Therefore the dreams of the great soul are not mere dreams ; they are positive indications of what can be done, of what will be done ; they are glimpses of the splendors of a greater day.

The soul that can rise to the mountain tops and see the splendor of greater things can indeed rejoice with great joy for such a soul is not destined for an ordinary life. Greater things are at hand and a wonderful future will positively be realized. But such a future, with its richer possibilities and its more worthy attainments, will not come back to us where we now stand. We must move forward and work for what we have seen in the vision. That which is greater does not come back to that which is lesser. We must press on into the life of the greater if we would realize such a life. And if we dreamed the dreams of the great soul those dreams will indicate that we can. What we have seen on the heights reveals what we can do if we will. We have gained the power; the gates are ajar, and in the beautiful somewhere our own is waiting.